# First World War
and Army of Occupation
# War Diary
France, Belgium and Germany

55 DIVISION
166 Infantry Brigade
Loyal North Lancashire Regiment
1/5th Battalion (Territorial Force)
1 January 1916 - 31 January 1918

WO95/2929/1

The Naval & Military Press Ltd
www.nmarchive.com
**Published in association with The National Archives**

Published by

## The Naval & Military Press Ltd

Unit 10 Ridgewood Industrial Park,

Uckfield, East Sussex,

TN22 5QE England

Tel: +44 (0) 1825 749494

www.naval-military-press.com

www.nmarchive.com

*This diary has been reprinted in facsimile from the original. Any imperfections are inevitably reproduced and the quality may fall short of modern type and cartographic standards.*

© **Crown Copyright**
**Images reproduced by permission of The National Archives, London, England, 2015.**

# Contents

| Document type | Place/Title | Date From | Date To |
|---|---|---|---|
| Heading | WO95/2929/1 1/5 Bn. Loyal N. Lancs Regt 1916 Jan-1918 Jan (Catalogue Says 1917 Dec) Will be amended | | |
| Heading | 55th Division 166th Infy Bde 1-5th Bn Loyal Nth Lancs Regt Jan 1916-Dec 1917 | | |
| Heading | 1/5 L.N Lancs Regt. Feb Vol VII | | |
| Heading | 1/5th L. N. Lancs Jan Vol VI | | |
| War Diary | Steenwerck Parts of A9.8.14.15 & 4 Sheet 36 | 01/01/1916 | 09/01/1916 |
| War Diary | Vergies, Somme | 12/01/1916 | 30/01/1916 |
| War Diary | Vergies | 01/02/1916 | 05/02/1916 |
| War Diary | Somme | 06/02/1916 | 12/02/1916 |
| War Diary | Bellacourt | 12/02/1916 | 29/02/1916 |
| War Diary | Bellacourt And Trenches From XI Central through X2a to X2b.3.6 Map 51c France | 01/03/1916 | 10/04/1916 |
| War Diary | Bellacourt | 11/04/1916 | 28/04/1916 |
| War Diary | France | 29/04/1916 | 30/04/1916 |
| War Diary | Trenches W. 12b6.4 To X1c 3 1/2.9 3/4 Map 51c Trenches T133 To T140 | 01/05/1916 | 05/05/1916 |
| War Diary | Trenches-W12b6.4 To X1b 10. 71/2 Map 51c | 06/05/1916 | 14/05/1916 |
| War Diary | Bellacourt Pas-De-Calais | 14/05/1916 | 20/05/1916 |
| War Diary | Trenches W 12.b 6.4 To X 1b 10 7 1/2 Map 51c. | 21/05/1916 | 31/05/1916 |
| Miscellaneous | Herewith War Diary Of 1/5th Bn Loyal N Lancs Regt | 13/01/1916 | 13/01/1916 |
| War Diary | Gouy Pas-De-Calain | 01/06/1916 | 03/06/1916 |
| War Diary | Trenches W12b 6.4 To X 1b 10.7 1/2 Sheet 51c | 04/06/1916 | 11/06/1916 |
| War Diary | Bellacourt | 12/06/1916 | 14/06/1916 |
| War Diary | Trenches W.12b6.4 To X1b 10.7 1/2 Sheet 51c | 15/06/1916 | 20/06/1916 |
| War Diary | Bellacourt | 15/06/1916 | 20/06/1916 |
| War Diary | Trenches | 20/06/1916 | 28/06/1916 |
| Heading | 1/5th Battalion The Loyal North Lancashire Regiment July 1916 | | |
| Heading | War Diary Of The 1/5th Loyal North Lancashire Regt. 166th Infantry Brigade 55th (West Lancashire) Division For The Period 1st July.1916 To 31st July.1916. Vol 12 | | |
| War Diary | Nr Bellacourt | 01/07/1916 | 04/07/1916 |
| War Diary | Gouy | 05/07/1916 | 08/07/1916 |
| War Diary | Bellacourt | 09/07/1916 | 18/07/1916 |
| War Diary | Grande Rullecourt | 20/07/1916 | 20/07/1916 |
| War Diary | Brevillers | 21/07/1916 | 21/07/1916 |
| War Diary | Outrebois | 22/07/1916 | 22/07/1916 |
| War Diary | Beaumetz | 23/07/1916 | 25/07/1916 |
| War Diary | Ville Sur Ancre | 26/07/1916 | 27/07/1916 |
| War Diary | Nr. Meaulte | 28/07/1916 | 31/07/1916 |
| Heading | 1/5th Battalion Loyal North Lancashire Regiment August 1916 | | |
| Heading | War Diary Of The 1/5 Loyal North Lanc. R. For The Period 1st August To 31st August 1916 Vol 13 | | |
| War Diary | A.15.a.4.2. Sheet 62d NE 1/20000 France | 01/08/1916 | 07/08/1916 |
| War Diary | F.23.A. | 07/08/1916 | 07/08/1916 |
| War Diary | A.4.c.& d. | 08/08/1916 | 10/08/1916 |
| War Diary | F.22.c.&d | 10/08/1916 | 20/08/1916 |
| War Diary | Acheux | 20/08/1916 | 31/08/1916 |

| | | | |
|---|---|---|---|
| Heading | War Diary Of 1/5th N. Lancs R. 1st September To 30th September 1916 Vol 14 | | |
| War Diary | Area E 12a Sheet 62d NE | 01/09/1916 | 06/09/1916 |
| War Diary | Trenches N.E. Edge Delville Wd | 06/09/1916 | 10/09/1916 |
| War Diary | Trenches | 11/09/1916 | 18/09/1916 |
| War Diary | N.31.b.6.0. (57 Cs.W.) | 19/09/1916 | 27/09/1916 |
| War Diary | Bivouac Pommier Redoubt | 27/09/1916 | 30/09/1916 |
| Heading | War Diary Of 1/5th N. Lan. Regt. For The Period 1st To 31st October 1916 Vol 15 | | |
| War Diary | Eaucourt, Somme. | 01/10/1916 | 02/10/1916 |
| War Diary | Proven, Belgium | 03/10/1916 | 06/10/1916 |
| War Diary | Trenches, Ypres. | 07/10/1916 | 31/10/1916 |
| Heading | War Diary Of 1/5th N. Lan R. For Period 1st November To 30th November 1916 Vol 16 | | |
| War Diary | Trenches Ypres C. 28.a.70.10 to C.29.b.25.25 Reference Map Secret W.L.19. | 06/11/1916 | 19/11/1916 |
| War Diary | Trenches Ypres. | 21/11/1916 | 30/11/1916 |
| Heading | War Diary Of 1/5th N. Lan. R For Period December 1st-31st 1916. Vol 17 | | |
| War Diary | Trenches St. Jean. C.28.a. 70.10. To C.29.b. 25.25 Secret Map W.L.19. | 01/12/1916 | 31/12/1916 |
| Heading | War Diary Of The 1/5 N. Lan. R For The Period 1/1/17 To 31/1/17 Vol 18 | | |
| War Diary | Yser Canal. Bank Ypres. | 01/01/1917 | 01/01/1917 |
| War Diary | Trenches | 02/01/1917 | 31/01/1917 |
| Miscellaneous | Preliminary Report On Raid | 10/01/1917 | 10/01/1917 |
| Miscellaneous | 55th Division No.1443/21 | 11/01/1917 | 11/01/1917 |
| Miscellaneous | 55th Division No.1443/24 G | 11/01/1917 | 11/01/1917 |
| Heading | War Diary Of 1/5 N Lan. R for the Period 1st To 28th February 1917 Vol 19 | | |
| War Diary | Volkerinckhove | 01/02/1917 | 02/02/1917 |
| War Diary | D Camp, Brandhoek | 02/02/1917 | 16/02/1917 |
| War Diary | Ypres, Canal Bank | 16/02/1917 | 21/02/1917 |
| War Diary | Trenches C28.a.70.10 C29.b.25.25 Secret Map W.L.19 | 21/02/1917 | 25/02/1917 |
| War Diary | B Camp, Brandhoek. | 25/02/1917 | 01/03/1917 |
| Heading | War Diary Of The 1/5th N Lan R For The Period 1st To 31st March 1917. Vol 20 | | |
| War Diary | B Camp, Brandhoek | 01/03/1917 | 06/03/1917 |
| War Diary | Convent, Ypres | 07/03/1917 | 16/03/1917 |
| War Diary | Prison, Ypres. | 16/03/1917 | 23/03/1917 |
| War Diary | Trenches C.28.a.70.10 C.29.b.25.25. Secret Map W.L.19. | 23/03/1917 | 29/03/1917 |
| Heading | War Diary Of 1/5th N. Lan. R. for the Period April 1st To 30th 1917 Vol 21 | | |
| War Diary | B Camp Brandhoek | 01/04/1917 | 07/04/1917 |
| War Diary | Convent, Ypres. | 07/04/1917 | 12/04/1917 |
| War Diary | Potijze | 12/04/1917 | 17/04/1917 |
| War Diary | Prison, Ypres. | 17/04/1917 | 22/04/1917 |
| War Diary | Wieltje Sector | 22/04/1917 | 27/04/1917 |
| War Diary | Prison, Ypres. | 27/04/1917 | 27/04/1917 |
| Heading | War Diary Of 1/5th N. Lan. R. for the Period May 1st To 31st 1917 Vol 22 | | |
| War Diary | Ypres. | 01/05/1917 | 31/05/1917 |
| Heading | War Diary Of 1/5th N. Lan. R. for the Period June 1st To June 30th 1917. Vol 23 | | |
| War Diary | Railway Wood | 01/06/1917 | 30/06/1917 |

| | | | |
|---|---|---|---|
| War Diary | Acquin V.1b-V.21-V22. Ref Map France No.27a SE | 01/07/1917 | 06/07/1917 |
| War Diary | Setques | 06/07/1917 | 20/07/1917 |
| War Diary | Query Camp | 21/07/1917 | 23/07/1917 |
| War Diary | Wieltje | 24/07/1917 | 31/07/1917 |
| Heading | War Diary Of The 1/5 N. Lan R. For The Period 1st July To 31st July 1917 Vol 24 | | |
| Heading | War Diary Of The 1/5 N. Lan R. For The Period 1st To 31st August1917 Vol 25 | | |
| War Diary | Trenches C.23.c | 01/08/1917 | 01/08/1917 |
| War Diary | Belgium Sheet 28 NW | 01/08/1917 | 01/08/1917 |
| War Diary | Wieltje Defences C.28.b Belgium. Sheet 28 NW | 02/08/1917 | 03/08/1917 |
| War Diary | Camp Near Watou | 04/08/1917 | 06/08/1917 |
| War Diary | Recques J.10.c And Sheet 27 NE France | 06/08/1917 | 31/08/1917 |
| Heading | War Diary Of The 1/5 N. Lan R. For The Period 1st To 30th Sept 1917 Vol 26 | | |
| War Diary | Recques J.10 C & D Sheet 27 NE France | 01/09/1917 | 13/09/1917 |
| War Diary | Canal Bank Ypres. | 14/09/1917 | 22/09/1917 |
| War Diary | Watou No.2 Area | 23/09/1917 | 24/09/1917 |
| War Diary | Beaulencourt France | 26/09/1917 | 28/09/1917 |
| War Diary | Longavesnes | 29/09/1917 | 29/09/1917 |
| War Diary | Trenches Ref Map Trench Map1/10,000 B.H.Q X15.b 80.60. From X17 Central To X10.0.98.60 | 30/09/1917 | 30/09/1917 |
| Heading | War Diary Of The 1/5 N. Lan R. For The 1st To 31st. October 1917. Vol 27 | | |
| War Diary | Trenches Honnecourt Left Sub Sector. Ref. Map France Sheet 57c SE 1/20000 | 01/10/1917 | 03/10/1917 |
| War Diary | X.17.b.00.20. to X.11.a.20.70. | 04/10/1917 | 13/10/1917 |
| War Diary | Longavesnes Ref. Map France Sheet 62c 1/40000 E.25.b. | 13/10/1917 | 22/10/1917 |
| War Diary | Trenches Honnecourt Ref.Map France Sht. 57c SE. X.17.b.00.20. To X.11.a.20.70. | 22/10/1917 | 28/10/1917 |
| War Diary | Trenches | 28/10/1917 | 28/10/1917 |
| Heading | War Diary Of The 1/5 Lan R For The Period 1st To 30th November 1917 Vol 28 | | |
| War Diary | Trenches Honnecourt Centre Sub-Sector | 01/11/1917 | 01/11/1917 |
| War Diary | Vaucellette Fm | 02/11/1917 | 09/11/1917 |
| War Diary | Trenches Honnecourt Centre Sub-Sector | 10/11/1917 | 30/11/1917 |
| Heading | War Diary Of The 1/5 Lan R For The Period 1st To 31st December 1917 Vol 29 | | |
| War Diary | 14 Willows Ref Map Villerc-Cuislain 1/10000 57c SE 4 | 01/12/1917 | 02/12/1917 |
| War Diary | Buire | 03/12/1917 | 05/12/1917 |
| War Diary | Flamicourt | 06/12/1917 | 07/12/1917 |
| War Diary | Noyelle Avion | 08/12/1917 | 10/12/1917 |
| War Diary | Chelers | 11/12/1917 | 11/12/1917 |
| War Diary | Troisvaux | 12/12/1917 | 12/12/1917 |
| War Diary | Fontaine Les Bourlans | 13/12/1917 | 14/12/1917 |
| War Diary | Erny St Julien | 15/12/1917 | 31/12/1917 |
| Heading | War Diary Of The 1/5 Lan R For The Period 1st To 31st January 1918 Vol 30 | | |
| War Diary | Erny St Julien | 01/01/1918 | 31/01/1918 |

WO 95 2929/1

1/5 Bn. Loyal N. Lancs Regt
1916 Jan – 1916 Jan (catalogue says
1917 Dec)
– will be
amended

55TH DIVISION
166TH INFY BDE

1-5TH BN LOYAL NTH LANCS REGT
JAN 1916 - DEC 1917

From 50 Div
151 BDE

To 57 Div 170 BDE

55

1/5 L.N Lancs Regt
Feb
Vol VII

Jan 1916

1/5th C.N. Lancers

55 166/55

Jan / Vol VI

Army Form C. 2118

1/5th L.N. Lancs. R
WAR DIARY
or
INTELLIGENCE SUMMARY
(Erase heading not required.)

| Place | Date | Hour | Summary of Events and Information | Remarks and references to Appendices |
|---|---|---|---|---|
| Paris of Ag 8, 16, 15 + 14 STEENWERCK | 1st January | | Still in billets. Inter Platoon Competition completed. Winning Platoon - No. 8. O.B. Coy. Platoon Commander Lieut Hy. Butterworth. | |
| | 2nd Jany | | Major Potter returned for duty from leave. Extract from Supplement to London Gazette dated 1/1/16.- Major (Temp. Lt. Col.) G. McHeath Coyt. (Temp. Major) B.B.O. Read 2/Lieut (Temp. Lieut.) H. Horrocks No 4730 C.S.M. W.R. Parker 1434 Sgt. J.T. Ball. Mentioned on Sir J.D.P. French's despatch 15-10-15 for "Gallant and Distinguished conduct in the Field". | |
| | 3rd Jany | | 3 Officers (2nd Lieuts) A Kenyon, Jnr. Blackburn & B. Slater, joined battalion for duty from England. | |
| | 6th Jany. | | Lt. Butterworth and 14 other ranks proceeded as billeting party to LONGPRE. | |
| | 8th Jany | | Battalion paraded at 5.30 pm and marched to BAILLEUL for entrainment. Lt. Chapman joined battalion at BAILLEUL station. Battalion left BAILLEUL 9-10 pm. | |
| | 9th Jany. | | Battalion arrived at PONT REMY at 5.10 am and at 6.15 am strength commenced march for billets at VERGIES, actually marching 29 Officers, + 700 other ranks. A.B.C. + Hd. Qrs. billeted at VERGIES, D Coy. + Machine Gunners billeted at LE FAY. | |

# WAR DIARY or INTELLIGENCE SUMMARY

**Army Form C. 2118.**

| Place | Date | Hour | Summary of Events and Information | Remarks and references to Appendices |
|---|---|---|---|---|
| VERGIES, SOMME. | 12th January | | Brigadier General (L. Green-Wilkinson) inspected Battalion outside Company billets, and afterward interviewed:— | |
| | | | No. 2236 C.Q.M.S. Maguire ⎫ | |
| | | | " 2085 Sergt. Maguire ⎬ Applicants for Commissions. | |
| | | | " 2531 Sept. Loughran ⎪ | |
| | | | " 2580 L/Cpl. J.E. Woods ⎭ | |
| | 13th Jany. | | 396 L/Cpl. Lee  D Coy, 2479 Pte. G. Rule  C Coy, 1953 Pte. C. Archer B Coy, proceeded to HALLENCOURT for duty at Divisional H.Q. Name of Pte. Dann submitted for appointment as Observer R.F.C. | |
| | 14th Jany. | | No. 1394 Arm. Sergt. A. Turton (A.O.C.) and 2/Lt. 64 Pte. Hu. Parker "A" Coy. (Tailor) proceeded to D.A.D.O.S. 55th Division for employment. | |
| | | | No. 1450 Sgt. Maguire D Coy. proceeded to HATTE FLIXECOURT to take up an appointment as Instructor at III Army School. Received following maps from Brigade:— | |
| | | | 90 maps  N.W. EUROPE  Sheet 3  1/250,000. | |
| | | | 31  "  AMIENS  "  12  1/80,000 | |
| | | | 24  "  ABBEVILLE  "  11  1/80,000 | |
| | 15th January. | | 2374 a/Sgt. Whitedge C. B Coy. proceeded to III Army N.C.O.'s School at FLIXECOURT for course of instruction. | |
| | 16th January. | | 2348 Pte. Newson J. A Coy. proceeded to HALLENCOURT for duty at Divisional H.Qrs. Received notification of following Honours and Awards (supplement to London Gazette dated Jany. 14th 1916.):— | |
| | | | Major (temp. Lt. Col.) G. Tee Smith — to be Companion of the D.S.O. | |
| | | | Capt. (2nd Major) H.R. Potter — awarded the D.C.M. | |
| | | | 2835 R.S.M. A. Watts — awarded the D.C.M. | |
| | | | Capt. (temp. Major) L.G.) Pechen — awarded Military Cross | |
| | | | 2nd Lt. Cromwell — awarded Military Cross | |

# WAR DIARY
## or
## INTELLIGENCE SUMMARY.
*(Erase heading not required.)*

Army Form C. 2118.

| Place | Date | Hour | Summary of Events and Information | Remarks and references to Appendices |
|---|---|---|---|---|
| VERGIES - SOMME | 17th January 1916 | | No. 1896 Pte. H.O. Hodgson B.Coy. + 2501 Pte. A. Tyldesley C.Coy. detailed to report to O.C. 98 Coy. A.S.C. for duty as loaders. C.Coy. provided working party of 1 officer and 50 men for work with Pioneers at railway crossing S. of WIRY church. | |
| | 18th Jany. | | 1009 Sgt. I. Meakin B.Coy and 2583 Cpl. S. Farnworth C.Coy. proceeded to BLENDECQUES to undergo course at the Cadet School. B Coy. furnished party similar to one provided by C. Coy on 17th Jany. | |
| | 19th Jany. 20th Jany. | | 2/Lt. R.H. Taylor joined battalion from England. Posted to A Coy. No. 2229 Pte. L. Fury A.B.Coy and 2335 Pte. I. Walker B.Coy. proceeded to 33rd Division H.Q. for duty as fatigue men. 2/Lt. I. Allen joined battalion from England. Posted to C Coy. | |
| | 21st Jany. 22nd Jany. | | Capt. D.C. Dilling member of F.G.C.M. assembled at HALLENCOURT. 2/Lt. A.B. Ford joined battalion from England. Posted to A Coy. Draft of 208 other ranks joined battalion (108 from No. 3 Entrenching battalion, + 100 from No. 4 Entrenching Battalion.) 2/Lt. Dann and 6 other ranks proceeded to WISQUES for machine gun course. | |
| | 24th Jany. 1916. | | Draft inspected by Brigadier General. | |

Army Form C. 2118.

# WAR DIARY
## or
## INTELLIGENCE SUMMARY.
*(Erase heading not required.)*

| Place | Date | Hour | Summary of Events and Information | Remarks and references to Appendices |
|---|---|---|---|---|
| WERGIES SOMME | 25th January. | | No.1814 Pte. J.W. Evans proceeded to No. 2 Territorial Base pending discharge T.E. | |
| | 26th Jany. | | M.O. attended conference of Medical Officers at HALLENCOURT. | |
| | 27th Jany. | | No. 2085 Sergt. A. Maguire, interviewed by Divisional Commander at H.Q. of LIVERPOOL SCOTTISH, HEUCOURT. No. 2560 Pte. R. Wilson instructed to report at H.Q. of 14th Corps DOMART-EN-PONTHIEU for duty as clerk. | |
| | 29th Jany. | | Battalion paraded at 6-30 a.m. and marched to HALLENCOURT where the Corps Commander, Lord Cavan, inspected the 55th Division. Strength on parade: 23 officers & 782 other ranks (including transport) | |
| | 30th Jany. | | Corps Commander forwarded his farewell wishes to Division, Brigade, & Battalion Commanders. | |

C.H. Potter - Major
adjt 1/5 L.N. Lancs Regt.

1/5th L.N.LAN.R.

**WAR DIARY**
or
INTELLIGENCE SUMMARY
(Erase heading not required.)

Army Form C. 2118

Feb 1916

| Place | Date | Hour | Summary of Events and Information | Remarks and references to Appendices |
|---|---|---|---|---|
| VERGIES | 1st Feb | | Still in billets at VERGIES, SOMME. | |
| | 2nd Feb. | | Commanding Officer interviewed by Lord Derby at Brigade Headquarters. | |
| | 3rd Feb. | | Divisional Commander inspected Regimental Grenadiers and one Platoon from each Company billeted. | |
| | 4th Feb. | | Battalion paraded at road junction N.E. of VERGIES at 6-30 a.m. and marched off at 7 a.m. Order of march: Signallers, D.A.B.C. Grenadiers, Stretcher-bearers, Machine gunners. Route:- VERGIES. BD. JUNCTION N. OF HEUCOURT on main WIRY-ALLERY road, DREUIL and road N. of railway, LONGPRE-LES-CORPS-SAINTS. Battalion strength marching, 25 officers, 814 other ranks. Arrived LONGPRE 11 a.m. Billeted night in LONGPRE. | |
| | 5th Feb. | | Battalion paraded 8-40 a.m. in RUE DU MOULIN, LONGPRE, and marched off at 8-50 a.m. Order of march: Signallers, C.D.A.B. Grenadiers, Stretcher-bearers, Machine gunners, Transport. Route:- L'ETOILE, VILLE-LE-MARCELET, BERTAUCOURT. -DES-DAMES. 1-30 p.m. Arrived BERTAUCOURT. Billeted BERTAUCOURT the night. | |

Army Form C. 2118

1/5th Bn L.N.LAN.R.

# WAR DIARY
or
# INTELLIGENCE SUMMARY
(Erase heading not required.)

Instructions regarding War Diaries and Intelligence Summaries are contained in F.S. Regs., Part II and the Staff Manual respectively. Title Pages will be prepared in manuscript.

| Place | Date | Hour | Summary of Events and Information | Remarks and references to Appendices |
|---|---|---|---|---|
| SOMME 1916 | 6th Feby | | Battalion however at 8-40 a.m. in BERTRANCOURT facing E. and marched off at 9 a.m. Order of march:- Signallers, B,C,D,A, Grenadiers, Stretcher-bearers, machine gunners, Transport. Route:- CANAPLES - BERNAVILLE. Arrived BERNAVILLE 12-15 p.m. Battalion billeted in BERNAVILLE until further orders. | |
| | 7th Feby | | No. 2470 Pte. R.W. Robinson D Coy. proceeded to DOMART to report to Divisional Theatre officer. | |
| | 9th Feby | | Major Potter proceeded by motor to inspect trenches which 166th Brigade will take over from the French. | |
| | 10th Feby | | Battalion paraded at 9 a.m. in BERNAVILLE facing E. Order of march:- Signallers A,B,C,D, Grenadiers, Stretcher-Bearers, machine gunners, 1st line Transport. Route:- BERNAVILLE, FIENVILLERS, HEM, DOULLENS, HALLOY. Arrived HALLOY 1-30 p.m., and stayed there in huts for the night. Strength marching 27 officers 827 other ranks. 3 other ranks reinforcement joined battalion. | |
| | 11th Feby | | Battalion paraded at 9 a.m. and marched via HALLOY, PAS, BRINCOURT, GAUDIEMPRÉ, POMMIER; and from POMMIER to BERLES AU BOIS, by platoons at 500 yards interval. Arrived BERLES AU BOIS at 2-30 p.m. and billeted night there. | |

Army Form C. 2118

1/5th Bn L.N. LAN. R.

# WAR DIARY
or
# INTELLIGENCE SUMMARY
(Erase heading not required.)

Instructions regarding War Diaries and Intelligence Summaries are contained in F.S. Regs., Part II. and the Staff Manual respectively. Title Pages will be prepared in manuscript.

| Place | Date | Hour | Summary of Events and Information | Remarks and references to Appendices |
|---|---|---|---|---|
| SOMME. | 19/6 12th Feby. | | Battalion paraded in BERLES AU BOIS at 5.30 a.m. and marched off at 100 yards intervals between platoons via BAILLEULMONT and BASSEUX to BELLACOURT. On arrival at BELLACOURT breakfasts were served in the village. About 10 a.m. whilst battalion was still in village waiting to takeover new trenches 15 German shells burst amongst our own men and the 1/10th Kings Liverpool (Scottish) Regt. and the following casualties occurred :— <br> 1357 Pte. Vanstone J. Coy. Killed. <br> 3422 " Greenhalgh J. "  Killed. (Grenadier.) <br> 2100 " McDonald J. A  Killed. ( do. ) <br> 2774 " Broughton J. C  Killed. ( top ) <br> 2233 LC Hasham J. " Wounded, head and hand (Gren) <br> 2082 Pte. Dixon J. " Wounded, ankle. -do- <br> 1783 " Taylor J. " Wounded, leg. -do- <br> 2706 " Fletcher W. " Wounded, leg. " <br> 1534 " King G. MO Wounded, leg. " <br> 2804 " Siff " MO Wounded, leg. thigh. chest " (Died same day.) <br> 2325 " Deaner L. D Wounded, ankle. <br> 2234 " Kirk G. " Wounded, wrist. <br> 2577 " Jumpset W. " Wounded, head. <br> 2362 " Gentlebury R. D Wounded, abdomen + R. leg. <br> 2058 " Bates W.G. A Wounded, back + spine <br> 1997 " Barton E. B Wounded, head. | |

Army Form C. 2118.

1/5th Bn. L.N.LAN.R.
WAR DIARY
or
~~INTELLIGENCE SUMMARY.~~
(Erase heading not required.)

Instructions regarding War Diaries and Intelligence Summaries are contained in F.S. Regs., Part II. and the Staff Manual respectively. Title pages will be prepared in manuscript.

| Place | Date | Hour | Summary of Events and Information | Remarks and references to Appendices |
|---|---|---|---|---|
| BELLACOURT 1916 | 12 Feby. (cont.) | | At 10-30 p.m. Battalion commenced to take over trenches from the French as follows:- A Coy. LE PARC, B Coy LA GRANGE, C Coy LES TROIS MAISONS, D Coy LES SAULES. The trenches were in muddy condition. No casualties occurred during relief. About noon the enemy shelled LES SAULES and the BELLACOURT communication trench, other trenches shelled slightly. Casualties:- 19974 L/S Hart W. A Coy. Wounded, shrapnel slight, about:- Our trenches are situate as follows:- E and S.E. of BELLACOURT from X1 central through R32c and 32d to R33a 4.1. 10th Royal Fusiliers - 111th Brigade, 37th Division - lay on our right and 1/10th Kings Liverpool (Scottish) Regt occupied line on our left. | Reference France 51c |
| | 13th Feby. | | Trenches still very muddy through continuous rain. Many cases of chilled feet, majority only slight. | |
| | 14th Feby. | | Trenches more wet and muddy than previous day. In some parts water reached the thighs; continuous baling and pumping had to be organised all along our line. A few further cases of chilled feet, mostly slight. 2783 Pte W. Todhunter B Coy. Wounded, shrapnel, eyehead. | |
| | 15th Feby. | | 397 pairs of gum-boots, thigh, reported late in the evening. Further cases of chilled feet reported, but a new supply of socks was available and distributed to men with slight feet, thus greatly reducing the numbers of what might have been serious cases. | |

1/5th Bn. Loyal N. Lancs. Regt.

**Army Form C. 2118.**

# WAR DIARY
or
# INTELLIGENCE SUMMARY.
(Erase heading not required.)

Instructions regarding War Diaries and Intelligence Summaries are contained in F.S. Regs. Part II. and the Staff Manual respectively. Title pages will be prepared in manuscript.

| Hour, Date, Place | Summary of Events and Information | Remarks and references to Appendices |
|---|---|---|
| BERLACOURT Feby 1916. 17th | 5th South Lancs. took over from us THE OSERIES, THE WILLOWS, and THE CHANGE trenches. 'A' Coy. remained in THE PARK, 'B' Coy. took over the support - LES SOUTIENS - 'C' & 'D' Coys. going into billets in BERLACOURT | |
| 18th Feby 1916. | Nos 126 & Pte Reynolds S. 'A' Coy. and 1271 Pte. Parkinson No. 'B' Coy. proceeded to ROUEN finding discharge TIME EXPIRED 18th March 16 | |
| 19th Feby 1916 | 'A' Coy. relieved 'C' Coy. in THE PARK trench and 'B' relieved 'D' -- in THE GRANGE trench 'C' and 'D' Coys. occupying the billets vacated by 'A' and 'B' Coys. No. 826. Pte M. Coleman died on 1/3rd M'SEX Field Ambulance. This man was admitted on 17th July, suffering from "vomiting and fever". | |
| 20th Feby 1916. | 'B' Coy. working during evening under R.E. 'D' Coy. moved from LES SOUTIENS to THE GRANGE relieving one Coy. of 1/5th South Lancs. Rgt. THE PARK and THE GRANGE now formed "night sector" and to be considered our sector until further orders. Two companies to occupy sector at a time. The other two companies to their respective billets in BERLACOURT. | |

1/5th Bn. Loyal N. Lancs. Regt.

Army Form C. 2118.

# WAR DIARY
## or
## INTELLIGENCE SUMMARY.
(Erase heading not required.)

Instructions regarding War Diaries and Intelligence Summaries are contained in F.S. Regs., Part II. and the Staff Manual respectively. Title pages will be prepared in manuscript.

| Hour, Date, Place | Summary of Events and Information | Remarks and references to Appendices |
|---|---|---|
| BELLACOURT 21st Feby 1916 | A Coy wounded working party of half Coy under 2nd Lt. Ernest Blackburn. Two disabled/wounded under 2nd Lt. Ernest Blackburn for LEWIS machine gun instruction. | |
| 22nd Feby 1916 | Capt. P.C. Dilling, member of 2/glam. (enlisted at York) 1/10th Lincolns. (Scottish Regt.) 2544. Pte. D.J. Shedding B. Coy, proceeded to Gov. to assist in Divisional Canteen. Snow fell though not heavily. Two men of C. Coy. 1520 Pte. Taylor J. and 1912 Pte. R. Pilchester brought three German prisoners into our lines about 10 pm. The prisoners were of good physique – 2 particulary – and of smart appearance. They surrendered very meekly to our men, and complained of being "fed up". A guard of 1 officer, 2/Lt Hogginson, and 4 other ranks escorted them to Brigade H.Q. | |

Army Form C. 2118.

# WAR DIARY
## or
## ~~INTELLIGENCE~~ SUMMARY.
(Erase heading not required.)

Instructions regarding War Diaries and Intelligence Summaries are contained in F.S. Regs., Part II. and the Staff Manual respectively. Title pages will be prepared in manuscript.

1/7th Northumbrian ?

| Hour, Date, Place | Summary of Events and Information | Remarks and references to Appendices |
|---|---|---|
| Ailiacourt 23rd Feby 1916 | Col. Sawyer, Comdg 3rd Line Northumbrian Division, on behalf of course of instruction from England conducted round trenches by Major Potter. A Coy and B Coy relieved C and D Coy on THE PARK and THE GRANGE respectively. C and D Coys went into Reserve billets. More snow fell. The following N.C.O.'s and men proceeded to 3rd Army School for trench mortar course:— 1355 Corpl. Cawton J. B. 2017 Pte. Spoller S. B. 2471 " Speakley A. J. B. 3177 " Taylor E. A. No.2389 Pte. J. Ashworth D Coy. proceeded to Divisional H.Q. for a course of "Mincers" instruction. No.1273 Pte H. Kane A Coy proceeded to No.2 Territorial Base, pending discharge TIME EX. C Coy. working under Signal Officer laying wire during evening | |
| 24th Feby/16. | | |
| 25th Feby 1916. | | |

Army Form C. 2118.

1st Bn Loyal N Lancs Regt

# WAR DIARY
## or
## INTELLIGENCE SUMMARY.
(Erase heading not required.)

Instructions regarding War Diaries and Intelligence Summaries are contained in F.S. Regs., Part II. and the Staff Manual respectively. Title pages will be prepared in manuscript.

| Hour, Date, Place | Summary of Events and Information | Remarks and references to Appendices |
|---|---|---|
| BETHUNE COURT. 26th Feby 1916. | A Coy provided working party under Signal Officer during evening burying wire. | |
| 27th Feby 1916 | C and D Coys relieved A and B Coys in THE PARK and THE GRANGE respectively. Divisional commander congratulated 2/Lt Hargreaves upon his patrol report rendered 25/2/16. | |
| 28 Feby '16 | About midnight 28/29th Feby 2/Lt Hargreaves and party of 8 Regtl. Grenadiers and 3 scouts detached and successfully bombed German listening post in X.2.a. (trench map RANSART). Party returned safely. | |
| 29th Feby 1916 | Brigadier General interviewed 2/Lt Hargreaves in B Coy officers billet. | |

C.R. Rothen. Major.
Cmdg 1/5 Loyal North Lancashire Regt.

# March 1916

**1/3rd N. Lancs R[?]**

## WAR DIARY / INTELLIGENCE SUMMARY

Army Form C. 2118

| Place | Date | Hour | Summary of Events and Information | Remarks and references to Appendices |
|---|---|---|---|---|
| BELLACOURT and trenches from X1 central through X2 a to X2 b 2. 6. Map. 51c France. | March 1st | | 2 Coys. in billets and 2 Coys. in trenches. 111th Brigade 37th Division on our right. 1/5th Bn. South Lancs. Regt. on our left. | |
| | March 2nd | | A. & B. Coy. relieved C. & D. Coy. in PARK and GRANGE trenches respectively. Capt. W. Whitehead rejoined battalion from II Corps striking school. II Corps intelligence renewed:- <br>2374 Sergt. Rothersides B. Coy. <br>3604 L/Cpl. A. Young D. " <br>2453 Pte. C.J. Barrett B. " <br>at Brigade HQrs. 6 p.m. reconnaissance. | |
| | March 3rd | | Lt. W.A. Richardson and 8 other ranks proceeded to WISQUES for course of instruction on LEWIS gun. Received 284 pairs of gum boots thigh from brigade Headquarters. | |
| | March 4th | | 10 other ranks reinforcement joined Battalion from 55th Division Base Depot. | |

# WAR DIARY
## 1/5th Bn Man. R.

~~INTELLIGENCE SUMMARY~~

(Erase heading not required.)

Army Form C. 2118

Instructions regarding War Diaries and Intelligence Summaries are contained in F.S. Regs, Part II. and the Staff Manual respectively. Title Pages will be prepared in manuscript.

| Place | Date | Hour | Summary of Events and Information | Remarks and references to Appendices |
|---|---|---|---|---|
| BELLACOURT and trenches from X1 central through X2a to X26.3.6. map 51c France | 1916 March 5th | | Two Coys. in billets, and 2 Coys. in trenches Our Artillery "straped" BLOCKHOUSE in German lines facing the WIDOWS trench, and also trenches around BLOCKHOUSE. The enemy Artillery did not retaliate. No. 2585 L/Cpl. Farnworth, gazetted 2nd Lieutenant, 1/5th Bn. Loyal North Lancashire Regt. | |
| | March 6th | | No. 1271 L/Cpl. Lya Lloyd proceded to 55th Division Base Dépôt ROUEN, pending discharge. TIME EXPIRED. C + D Coys relieved A + B Coys in the PARK and GRANGE trenches respectively. | |
| | March 9th | | No. 2631 L/Cpl. Jo. Ingham. 'A' Coy. proceded to England; to report to I.F.3. War Office pending course of instruction at the Cadet School, prior to appointment to commission in 3/4th East Lancashire Regt. 2 Lt. A.G. Rann | |
| | March 10th | | A + B Coys. relieved C + D Coys. in the PARK and GRANGE respectively. 2/Lt. J. Farnworth joined Battalion for duty. | |

Army Form C. 2118

1/5th Bn. L.N. Lan. R.

# WAR DIARY
## INTELLIGENCE SUMMARY
*(Erase heading not required.)*

Instructions regarding War Diaries and Intelligence Summaries are contained in F. S. Regs., Part II. and the Staff Manual respectively. Title Pages will be prepared in manuscript.

| Place | Date | Hour | Summary of Events and Information | Remarks and references to Appendices |
|---|---|---|---|---|
| BELLACOURT and trenches from X.1.central through X.2.a to X.26.36 Map 51.c. March | 1916 | | Two companies in Bellacourt and two companies in trenches. | |
| | 11th March 1916 | | No. 1297 Cpl. C.J. Buckley proceeded to 35th Division Base Depot, ROUEN, pending discharge T.E. 2/Lt. H.A. Richardson and party returned LEWIS gun course at WISQUES. | |
| | 12th March 13th March | | Lt. Col. G. Heckell returned from sick leave. No. 840. C.Q.M.S. J. Kay proceeded to 35th Division Base Depot ROUEN, pending discharge T.E. | |
| | 14th March | | Germans sent 3 shells into BELLACOURT. One burst in yard of Battalion Red Xy about 6 pm. one wounded. No. 508. Pte. J. Bolton B. Coy. Shrapnel back. C & D Coys. relieved A & B Coys. in PARK and GRANGE respectively | |
| | 15th March | | The following N.C.O's. and men proceeded to Base, pending discharge TIME EXPIRED.<br>No. 2r. C/Sgt. Jackson J. 39 Pnr. Sgt. Buckley C.<br>71 Sgt. Farrington M. 291 Sgt. [illegible] W.J.<br>271 Pte. Scott J. 197 Pte. Goody W.<br>871 " Vickers A. 183 " Vose W.<br>No. 2236 C.Q.M.S. May J. also proceeded to l'ARBRET en route for England to thank to I.F.3 War Office, pending appointment to Commission. | |

1875  Wt. W593/826  1,000,000  4/15  J.B.C. & A.  A.D.S.S./Forms/C. 2118.

**Army Form C. 2118**

1/5th Bn. London Regt.

# WAR DIARY
## or
## INTELLIGENCE SUMMARY
*(Erase heading not required.)*

| Place | Date | Hour | Summary of Events and Information | Remarks and references to Appendices |
|---|---|---|---|---|
| BELLACOURT and trenches from X.1 central through X.2.a to X.2.b Map 51c France | 1915/16 | | Two companies in billets and 2 companies in trenches. | |
| | 16th March | | No. 4th Cadn. Windn. V.J. and 1297 Pte R.A. Scrogg proceeded to Base pending discharge time expired. 10th the nar to reinforcement joined Battalion from 33rd Division Base Depot. | |
| | 17th March | | 6 officers and 60 other ranks attended "FLAMMENWERFER" demonstration at BEAUMETZ. | |
| | 18th March | | A. & B. Coys. relieved C. & D. Coys. in PARK and GRANGE trenches respectively. | |
| | 21st March | | No. 2580 L/Cpl. J.W. Woods proceeded to Cadet School BLENDECQUES for course of instruction. No. 2574 L/Cpl. S. Marley proceeded to England for course at a Cadet School pending granting of commission in 3/19th London Regt. | |
| | 22nd March | | C. & D. Coys. marched to SAULTY arriving there about 10.15 pm. after being relieved in trenches by 19 Coys. 5th South Staffs. A. & B. Coys. billeted nightly in BELLACOURT. 10 other ranks attached 421 St French Mortar Battery for instruction. 1 N.C.O. & 1 officer (Lt. Richardson) and 61 other ranks remained in BELLACOURT to work under Brigade | |

# WAR DIARY
## INTELLIGENCE SUMMARY
*(Erase heading not required.)*

Army Form C. 2118

Instructions regarding War Diaries and Intelligence Summaries are contained in F.S. Regs., Part II. and the Staff Manual respectively. Title Pages will be prepared in manuscript.

| Place | Date | Hour | Summary of Events and Information | Remarks and references to Appendices |
|---|---|---|---|---|
| SAULTY - DE-CALAIS | | | A. & B. Coys marched from BELLACOURT, arriving at SAULTY 1-15 p.m. | |
| | March 23rd | 10 p.m. | No. 2751 Pte. H. Jowell despatched to Base. Under age. | |
| | | | " 4514 L/Sgt. S. Barnett proceeded to Base. T.E. | |
| | March 24th | | No. 1323 Pte. J.H. Morh proceeded to Base T.E. | |
| | March 25th | | " 3843 Pte. J. Westwood C. Coy proceeded to Base. Under age. | |
| | March 26th | | 2435 Cpl. I. Watson attended 55th Division School for Antigas Course. | |
| | March 27th | | No. 1282 Pte. J. Hutchinson proceeded to 55th Division Base Depot, pending discharge. TIME EXPIRED. | |
| | | | No. 1695 Pte. J. McLew reported to Camp Commandant 55th Division for employment in Division Barbers Shop. | |
| | | | 2nd/Lt. Cecil Brown Coldham and draft of 51 other ranks joined battalion from 55th Division Base Depot. | |
| | March 28th | | 1988 Pte. W. Winterbottom and 3694 Pte. W. Greenwood proceeded to 55th Division, GOUY for employment in Canteen. | |
| | March 29th | | No. 2383 L/Cpl. R. Pye interviewed by Brigadier General at Brigade H.Q. at 5-30 p.m. re commission. | |

1/5th L.N. Lancs R.

**WAR DIARY** or **INTELLIGENCE SUMMARY**

Army Form C. 2118

| Place | Date | Hour | Summary of Events and Information | Remarks and references to Appendices |
|---|---|---|---|---|
| SAULTY and BELLACOURT. 2 Coys in trenches from X1 central through X2a to X2b. 3.6 Map 51c France. | 30th March | | A and B Coys left SAULTY, marching at 100 yards intervals between platoons via ARBRET, BAILLEULMONT, and BASSEAUX to BELLACOURT arriving about 5.15 p.m. Took over billets from 2 Coys 5th South Lancs. C + D Coys left SAULTY 4 p.m. proceeding by same route had marching in same formation as A + B Coys. Took over trenches from 2 Coys 5th South Lancs. C Coy. occupying PARK and B Coy. GRANGE. | |
| | 31st March | | No. 1463 L/Cpl. Warren D Coy. proceeded to GOUY for course at 55th Division aiming school. No. 2946 L/Cpl. R. Milne interviewed by Brigadier-General at Brigade H.Q. at 5.30 p.m. re Commission. | |

W. Long Lt.
Adjt. 1/5th L.N. Lanc R
5-4-16

1/5th Bn. Loyal N. Lancs. Regt.
April 1916

Army Form C. 2118.

# WAR DIARY
## INTELLIGENCE SUMMARY.
(Erase heading not required.)

| Place | Date | Hour | Summary of Events and Information | Remarks and references to Appendices |
|---|---|---|---|---|
| BETHUNE COURT Trenches X.1 centre through X.2.a.d.X.2.b.3.b Ref. Map France 51a | 1916 1st AM. | | Two companies in trenches PARK and GRANGE. Two companies in billets in BETHUNE COURT. 12th Brigade - 4th Divison on our right. 1/5th South Lancs. Regt. on our left. H.Q. of Kenyon left for HAVRÉ to undergo a months course at the transport school. | |
| | 2nd AM. | | No 145 A Kenyon and Donald enlisted and posted to Base and proceed to Base time to Kay proceed to 3rd Army School, previous course of instruction. | |
| | 3rd Apl. | | 2976 L/Cpl A. Dickson interviewed by Brigadier General. Application for commission. Draft of 49 other ranks reinforcement arrived from 3rd Division Base Depot. | |
| | 5th AM. 8th AM. | | A + B Coys relieved C + D Coys in PARK + GRANGE respectively. Hostilities by Major G.H. Totnianand of Buckingham Palace To His Majesty The King at Buckingham appointed as Comd to Lt Col J.B. Thompson School | |
| | 9th AM. | | 3151 Pte Jenning & 2850 Pte a during sgt 2/50 Gunner to Surmance at ARBRET w farquence | |
| | 10th AM. | | 2/Lt B.H. Leafer Gr.} To 55th Divisional School 2450 Sgt. Hunter Gr.} for course of instruction 289 J/S. Melia | |

1/5th L.N. LAN. R.

# WAR DIARY
## INTELLIGENCE SUMMARY
(Erase heading not required.)

Army Form C. 2118.

| Place | Date | Hour | Summary of Events and Information | Remarks and references to Appendices |
|---|---|---|---|---|
| BELLACOURT | 1916 | | | |
| | 11th April 1916 | 3h 42 | Shell 15" Trebby & Central through X 24.b.6.2 & 6.5 & by 12 Trebby flying to bursts; that & that offr twenty minus 5.45, 9 R and D. | |
| | | | Total 9 Toad. London Regiment attached for four days instruction in trenches | |
| | | | C. & D. Coys relieved A & B Coys in PARK and GRANGE respectively | |
| | 12th April 1916 | | Casualty No. 2162 Pte J. Tagg D Coy wounded by bomb. Fair shot – accidental | |
| | 13th April | 1.30 & 9.45 | We don't experienced by trigger over in ref. to application for commission | |
| | 14th April | | Notification sent to all officers and men on leave. Casualty 1679 Pte. Howard to wounded, bayonet, right arm, wounded in bayoneting fight, evacuated to his coy 15 of afternoon, returned to duty | |
| | 15th April | | Casualty 3105 Pte. P. Mulhern reports to Dr. wounded and taken off duty | |
| | | | 5 NCO's attended Lectures delivered by 5th Army Chemical Advisor on Post Respirator at GREMELLE | |
| | 16th April | 12.30 etc | W & C Coys proceeded to Barrel E aqueduct. Two Coys relieve by Battn houses working parties. Two raiding parties German trenches 500 yds, NY MONCHY at 9pm considerably raided, German artillery bombarding after W. & B. Coys relieved D Coy in PARK & GRANGE respectively | |

1/5th L'N'LAN R.

Army Form C. 2118.

# WAR DIARY
## INTELLIGENCE SUMMARY
(Erase heading not required.)

| Place | Date | Hour | Summary of Events and Information | Remarks and references to Appendices |
|---|---|---|---|---|
| BELLACOURT. Nymph 51.c. | 18th April | | Still in trenches X trench through X2 a 10x2 & 3.6. France. | |
| | | | 949 Cpl. Forrest, 1302 Pte W. Lewis, 1305 Pte. W. Niles proceeded to Base T.E. Lt. Col. Wickyth granted special leave from this date to Pte Burkhide, and Pte Young proceeded to England to take up commissions. | |
| | 19th April | | 6662 Pte W. Blue proceeded to Base. Under age. | |
| | 20th April | | 2085 Sgt. A. Maguire proceeded to 55th Divisional School of Instruction for duty as Instructor. | |
| | 22nd April | | 2410 Pte H. Gullivan joined Div. Theatre Coy. | |
| | 23rd April | | 5th South Lancs. Regt relieved A & D Coys in PARK and B RANGE A.C. Coys marched from BELLACOURT to billets at SAVLTY. D Coy went into billets at GOUY, and B Coy remain in BELLACOURT. | |
| | 24th April | | B Coy left BELLACOURT for billets at SAVLTY. | |
| | | | 2/Lt A. Kenyon returned from Transport course at HAVRE. | |
| | 25th April | | 629 Pte W Unworth R. went on a Transport course. | |
| | | | 1/55 Pte L. A. Saylor and 1328 Pte W. Bagneaux proceeded to Base - T. E. | |
| | 26th April | | B Co. + A Coys left SAVLTY for huts in GOUY. (P.16) ref 51c map. | |
| | 27th April | | Still at GOUY | |
| | 28th April | | Lt. Col. Greekyth returned from special leave. Casualty - 2282 Pte Doran Edwin killed. Slight at duty. | |

1/5th N. LAN R.

Army Form C. 2118.

# WAR DIARY
## INTELLIGENCE SUMMARY
(Erase heading not required.)

| Place | Date | Hour | Summary of Events and Information | Remarks and references to Appendices |
|---|---|---|---|---|
| France | 1916 29th April | | Battalion took over trenches T.140 to T.133 from 2nd Bn. Essex Regt. 12th Bde. 4th Division. C. Coy. allotted trenches T.133 to T.D.6.) W/12.6.6.4. to D " - " - " T.137 to T140) X/C.3½.6.34 B Coy remained at GOUY. A " " " " " over Support Line Lt Col. Yorkish proceeded to 3rd H.Q. headquarters AUXI-LE-CHATEAU to attend a conference. 2/Lts Ledsham and Reaton and 10/13 Sgt. I. Berkeley and 338th & 9 Usar attended course of instruction at Divisional School. Capt. A. Brindle and 366 Sgt A. Key returned from course at 3rd Army School. | |
| | 30th April | | B. Coy. moved from GOUY to billets in BELLACOURT. Casualty :- 440 Cpl. H. Jackson, G.S.W. right thigh | |

J. M. Loughrey
Lieut Col.
for Cmdg 1/5th L. N. Lan. Rgt.

May 1916

# WAR DIARY
## INTELLIGENCE SUMMARY

1/5th LN Lancs R.

| Hour, Date, Place | Summary of Events and Information | Remarks and references to Appendices |
|---|---|---|
| Trenches W.12 to G.14 to X.1.c.3b.9b - Huptote Trenches T.133.6 T.140 1st May 1916 | Still in trenches. 10th Bayou Artillery 110th Bde 37th Division on our right. | |
| 2nd May 1916 | 1322 Pte. Baberly and 1328 Staff matron proceeded to base sent sick. | |
| 3rd May | Capt. T. Gatwicke and 1st 53rd L/Cpl Lightfoot attended 37th Army School. AUXI-LE-CHATEAU for course of instruction. "D" Coy took over support line and "A" Coy went into trenches T.140 to T.144 (+ 1032.96 & x 160.75) | |
| 4th May | Aeroplanes stood to in trenches about 5am. Artillery of both sides bombarded trenches or re-balanced our own right for about an hour. No developments on our particular part of the line. Artillery quiet at dawn. | |
| 5th May | Casualties - 2509 Pte. Darling G.W. "A" Coy. shrapnel left hand slight wound. 2011 Pte. Thorpe J.H. "B" Coy. shrapnel, right thigh, slight, at duty | |

# 1/1st L.N.LAN.R.

## WAR DIARY or INTELLIGENCE SUMMARY

Army Form C. 2118.

| Hour, Date, Place | Summary of Events and Information | Remarks and references to Appendices |
|---|---|---|
| Trenches W.12 & 6.64 to X.1.6.10.74. Ref 51c. 6th May 1916. | 2224 Pte Pinkins J. and 2034 Pte. Pinkins S. detailed for duty as Orderlies at VI Corps H.Q. C.O. returned from Conference at III Army H.Q. Batalion moved from LARBRÉT to MONCHIET | |
| 7th May | 2396 Pte Mason and 1849 Pte Broughton joined 160th Bde. Machine Gun Corps for transport duty. 1097 Pte. J Darlington, 495 Pte J Leatherbarrow 1751 Pte. J Melling, 1160 Pte. J Haddon and 1110 Pte. Ayrton, R.A.M.C, attached proceeded to Base "Time expired". | |
| 8th May | 5236 Pte Turner joined 2nd Field Survey Coy. R.E. R.O.H. for duty as photographic worker. | |
| 9th May | 1326 Pte to Brewik To Base time ext. | |
| 10th May | 2383 H/c R.H. Rev. to VI Corps H.Q. for examination by Corps Doctor. Returned following day. News that Capt Pilling & Sgt Corpl. Rev. Wallace who were accidentally poisoned at Gout GOUY. have recovered and are attending Boxing Demonstration. | |

Army Form C. 2118.

# WAR DIARY
## or
## INTELLIGENCE SUMMARY.

(Erase heading not required.)

| Hour, Date, Place | Summary of Events and Information | Remarks and references to Appendices |
|---|---|---|
| 1916 | | |
| 11th May 1916. | 6.30 "B" On 11th hrs received C.T. and A enemy's trenches T.33 to T.79 inclusive. "B" Coy took over trenches temporarily - 6 Coys went into billets in BERTANCOURT. Casualties - 1172 Pte Jamieson A legs shrapnel. Any exposure. Eye wound. 1179 Pte Chisnall A leg. G.S.W. night inj. 1706 L/Cpl H Miles D-1 G.S.W. neck inj. | |
| 12th May 1916. | 1313 Sergt Emmengagh 1026 L/Cpl Sheridan and 10.99 Pte. G. Birch, + 338 Pte F. Miller to Base time expired. | |
| 13th May. | III Army Commander Gen'l Sir H. Allenby K.C.B. visited BERTANCOURT and inspected trenches held by 50th Division. | |
| 14th May. | The under mentioned proceeded to 4th Army Trench mortar school for course of instruction. 70 Bing Sparkes. 2334 M.C. Farrington, 5216 Pte. Quegan J. 5216 Pte Blackburn J. 2228 Pte Dunn. 1620 Loring J. W. (Servants) 2247 L/Cpl. Martell. No.96 Pte. Quegan J. 2901 Pte Blackburn J. 2022 Pte Harvey | |

1/5th N. LAN. R.

# WAR DIARY or INTELLIGENCE SUMMARY

Army Form C. 2118.

| Hour, Date, Place | Summary of Events and Information | Remarks and references to Appendices |
|---|---|---|
| BELLACOURT PAS-DE-CALAIS 14th May 1916 | A Draft joined Battalion. 1) Forty other ranks from 4th Lancashire Bde. 2) Three other ranks from 7th Bn Manchester Regt. 3) Nine other ranks from 55th Div. Base Depot. Total – 52 other ranks. | |
| 16th May 1916. | Major Potter, 9 N.C.O.s and 7 N.C.O.s attended lecture by 2nd in Command at the theatre, Gouy, on "Hand to Hand Fighting". In the afternoon the same party attended another Grenade demonstration at 8.19 a 9.9. Gouy. | |
| 17th May. | 2137 2/Lt. B. Ward & proceeded to Gouy for a course. | |
| 18th May. | 2137 2/Lt. B. Ward returned & 1767 2/Lt. S. Sutton with 1 Sgt/C. J. Parker, went to Divisional School for course of instruction. | |
| 20th May. | Battalion relieved 2 South Lancs Regt in trenches T.133 to T.144 inclusive. Disposition as follows:– Front Line, C. Coy. T.133 to T.136; B. Coy. T.137½ to T.140; A. Coy. T.141 to T.144; D. Coy. in Reserve | |

1/6 M Bn N. Lan R.

Army Form C. 2118.

# WAR DIARY
## or
## INTELLIGENCE SUMMARY.
*(Erase heading not required.)*

Instructions regarding War Diaries and Intelligence Summaries are contained in F.S. Regs., Part II. and the Staff Manual respectively. Title pages will be prepared in manuscript.

| Hour, Date, Place | Summary of Events and Information | Remarks and references to Appendices |
|---|---|---|
| Trenches W.12.b.6.4. to X.16.10.7b. Map 51c. 21st May 1916 | 10.35+ 2/c N. Fielding and 338 P/s M. Wareside proceeded to Base pending transfer to England. One expired. | |
| 22nd May | 2/Lt Vickers granted local leave to England. | |
| 24th May | 9.0 a.k. of 37 other ranks joined Battalion from no. 1 Entrenching Battalion. He also 103300 L/Sgt. Wye & 999 L/Cpl. Spencer attended course in Physical & Bayonet fighting at 55th Divisional School. | |
| 25th May | 2/Lt B. Longbottom M. Nelson joined Bn. from England. Casualties:- 3562 Pte. Whittle & N 606 G.S.W. L. cheek, 1530 Sgt. Bootle W. E. & 607 G.S.W. L. buttock, slight at duty. | |
| 26th May | Casualty. 3879 Pte. E. Green. Killed in Action. | |

1/5th N. LAN. R.

Army Form C. 2118.

# WAR DIARY
## or
## INTELLIGENCE SUMMARY.
*(Erase heading not required.)*

Instructions regarding War Diaries and Intelligence Summaries are contained in F.S. Regs., Part II. and the Staff Manual respectively. Title pages will be prepared in manuscript.

| Hour, Date, Place | Summary of Events and Information | Remarks and references to Appendices |
|---|---|---|
| Evening of 1916 of X.16 to 10.7K. & 10.51C. 27th May 1916. | 5th N Lanc. Regt. took over our trenches Battalion proceeded to huts at GOUY - in Divisional Reserve. 3 other ranks joined on from 1st Entg. Bn. | |
| 28th May 1916. | Lt. Col. Foster returned from special leave. | |
| 29th May 1916. | 1350 Lt Aimonough proceeded to Base pending transfer to England, some exposed. | |
| 30th May 1916. | Major to be Solan attended III Army school for concluding day of course for month of May. The following officers proceeded to England on leave - Capt E.W. Welch, 2/Lt J. Drinkall, 2/Lt C. Bain, 2/Lt J. Kearns ---  J.G. Frankland<br>2/Lt J. Faulkner | |
| 31st May 1916. | Nil - | |

L Longrigg. Lt. Col.
Comdg 1/5th N.Lancs Regt.

Oct 86

To Officer i/c
    Adj: Office.
        Base

Herewith War Diary of 1/5th
Bn Loyal N. Lancs. Regt. for
the month of June.

                    D. Long  Lieut for
                              Lt Col.
13/7/6      Cmdg 1/5. L.N. LANR

55

June 1916
1/5 LN Lancs Regt
Vol XI

Army Form C. 2118

# WAR DIARY
## or
## INTELLIGENCE SUMMARY
(Erase heading not required.)

| Place | Date | Hour | Summary of Events and Information | Remarks and references to Appendices |
|---|---|---|---|---|
| GOUY 7AS.J.E.CALAIS | 1916 1/6 | | Battalion in Divisional Reserve at GOUY. Major C.R. Shaw left Battalion. First day of Battalion Sports. | |
| " | 2/6 | | 2nd day of Battalion Sports. Final events guarded; at Brigade attended the N.C.Os. Small and 10 men joined 166th Bde. Machine Gun Coy. | |
| " | 3/6 | | Divisional Commander, Major Gen. H.S. Jeudwine C.B. inspected Battalion, examining various articles of equipment & of many of the N.C.Os and men. He reported well of the battalion | |
| Trenches W12.b 6.4 to X.6.10.7½ sheet 51c | 4/6 | | Battalion relieved 1/5th Bn. South Lancs Regt in trenches T133 to T144, as under;<br>B Coy. in LANARK - T133 to T136. Battalion of 37th Division on<br>D - LLANJAFF - T137 to T140. our immediate right, and<br>A - PARK - T141 to T144. a Battalion of our own Division<br>C - Reserve dugouts (the 55th) on our left.<br>Orderly Room Clerk, R.Q.M.S Herbert proceeded to Territorial Infantry Records Base, Rouen, for the purpose of comparing records. | |
| " | 5/6 | | Lieut A.R.B. killed twelve. Lieut. A.R.B. Chapman, killed in action. Battalion on our right - 10th Royal Fusiliers, attempted a raid on German trenches about 1 am.<br>No. 2801 Pte J. Blackburn, attached to 166/1 Trench Mortar<br>" 2245 " J. Dunn " " | |

Army Form C. 2118

# WAR DIARY
## or
## INTELLIGENCE SUMMARY
(Erase heading not required.)

Instructions regarding War Diaries and Intelligence Summaries are contained in F.S. Regs., Part II. and the Staff Manual respectively. Title Pages will be prepared in manuscript.

| Place | Date | Hour | Summary of Events and Information | Remarks and references to Appendices |
|---|---|---|---|---|
| Trenches W.12.b.6.4 to X.1.d.10.7½ Sheet 51.C. | 6/10 | | Draft of 46 other ranks joined Battalion from 55th Division Base. Draft "1" No. 4 Entrenching Battalion. 3429 Pte. I. Jackson "D" Coy. wounded. G.S.W. r. upper arm + forehead. No. 1 Jackson "D" Coy. wounded. | |
| " | 7/10 | | Brigadier inspected draft at 3.30 p.m. | |
| " | 8/10 | | Major C.K. Potter undertook duties of Commandant at 55th Divisional School. | |
| " | 10/10 | | No. 14614 Sgt. L. he hereby awarded course of instruction in S. Gravelin at Flying School. | |
| " | 11/10 | | Capt. P.C. Pilling and 1565 Sgt. H. Ashton "C" Coy. proceeded to III Army School for course of instruction. L/c. A.F. Marquand attached to 164th Infantry Brigade staff. | |
| BELLACOURT | 12/10 | | 246 L/Cpl. Curvis, 2143 L/Cpl. R. Whitley "B" Coy, 2579 L/Sgt. T. Barton, "A" Coy: proceeded to 55th Divisional School for course of instruction. Battalion relieved by 1/3 South Lancs. Regt. A, B, and D Coys went into billets in BELLACOURT and constituted Brigade Reserve. C Coy took over the SOUTIEN in support of 1/3 Kings Own (Rl.) Regt. | |
| " | 14/10 | | Daylight Saving Bill came into operation for the British Army in France. All clocks put forward one hour at 11 p.m. | |

# WAR DIARY
## or
## INTELLIGENCE SUMMARY
*(Erase heading not required.)*

Army Form C. 2118

| Place | Date | Hour | Summary of Events and Information | Remarks and references to Appendices |
|---|---|---|---|---|
| Trenches M.12.C.6.4 to X.18.10.7½ Sheet 51.C. and BELLACOURT. | 15/6 | | 2nd in Command – Capt. J. Entwistle – attended lecture at ARRAS on "Heavy Artillery". Lt. Col. Goldsmith performed the duties of Brigadier during afternoon and evening in the absence of Brigadier General L. Green Wilkinson. | |
| | 16/6 | | Battalion provided special carrying parties under R.E. Parties consisted of C.O. 12 officers and about 500 other ranks and parties continued into parties of 40. Each party reported at H.Qrs of 165th Brigade at intervals of ½ an hour between each, commencing about 9.30 pm. | Parties continued |
| " | 17/6 | | Special carrying parties again provided as for night of 16th. | |
| " | 18/6 | | Special carrying parties as per night of 16th. Casualties :- 6130 Pte R. Davies 1 Coy and 1782 Pte Spellman, B Coy, wounded, aeroplane bomb. | |
| | 19/6 20/6 | | No. 2382 L/Cpl. G. Quenby C Coy. proceeded to Cadet School for course of instruction. Battalion relieved 1/5 South Lancs in night stations. Coys. were allotted as under :- 
B Coy. LANARK – T133 to T136     1 Coy of 1/5th Bn.
D " LLANDAFF – T137 to T140     Kings Own (R.L.) Regt.
A " PARK – T141 to T144     in support
C " GRANGE – T145 to T148
Each Coy had 2 platoons in front line and 2 platoons in support line | |
| Trenches | | | | |

# WAR DIARY or INTELLIGENCE SUMMARY

Army Form C. 2118

| Place | Date | Hour | Summary of Events and Information | Remarks and references to Appendices |
|---|---|---|---|---|
| Trenches | 22/6 | | No. 14764 Sgt. Berkeley and 1770 Pte. Roscoe attended short course of "Wireless" at GOUY | |
| " | 23/6 | | Draft of 12 other ranks joined Battalion from 55th Division Base Depôt. Orderly Room Clerk - R.Q.M.S. Kenwick - rejoined Battalion from duty at Base. | |
| " | 24/6 | | 2/Lt. I. Aiken proceeded to G.H.Q. for Intelligence employment. Operation orders affecting 166th Bde. issued to Coys. at 8.30 a.m. A heavy bombardment to some distance to our right preceded throughout the day, and a less heavy bombardment took place on our Divisional left sector. Our own front was particularly quiet. Orders were issued that no men except on duty were to be allowed in BELLACOURT or GROSVILLE, and all soldiers and civilians were confined to their cellars during hours of daylight. No patrols were sent out night of 24/25. | |
| " | 26/6 | | 2 officers 2/Lt. C.E. Hadam and 2/Lt. B. Harding joined Battalion from England. Casualty:- 3205 Pte. J. Walsh D. Coy. G.S.W. under left eye. | |
| " | 27/6 | | 3046 Pte. A. Hadam C. Coy. wounded shrapnel, left buttock and groin. | |
| " | 28/6 | | Each battalion in 165th Brigade and 2 battalions of 164th Brigade conducted successful raids on enemy trenches facing WAILLY. Raids were carried out in daylight at 5 p.m. accompanied by gas and smoke barrage. 2022 Pte. J. Hamill attached 166th Trench Mortar Battery killed in action. Shrapnel, 1st finger right hand, slight to ..... Ord/Sgt 1/5th L.N. Lan R. | |

166th Brigade.
55th Division.

1/5th BATTALION

THE LOYAL NORTH LANCASHIRE REGIMENT

JULY 1 9 1 6

War Diary
of the
1/5th Loyal North Lancashire Regt,
166th Infantry Brigade,
55th (West Lancashire) Division
for the period
1st July, 1916 to 31st July, 1916.

**Army Form C. 2118**

# WAR DIARY
## or
## INTELLIGENCE SUMMARY
(Erase heading not required.)

Instructions regarding War Diaries and Intelligence Summaries are contained in F. S. Regs., Part II. and the Staff Manual respectively. Title Pages will be prepared in manuscript.

| Place | Date | Hour | Summary of Events and Information | Remarks and references to Appendices |
|---|---|---|---|---|
| N' Bellacourt | 1 July 1916 | | In Trenches T.133.b. T.148. W. B.6.4. to x 2 a. 10.18. (Sheet 51 C.) 37th Division on our immediate right. 1/10 Bn. Liverpool (Scottish) Regt. on our left. 'Z' day as per operation Orders, Appendix A. Smoke sent over at 7.30 am. No retaliation on our trenches by enemy artillery or infantry. News of 3rd and 4th Army assaults between GOMMECOURT and the SOMME received in dyn C in C Potter returned for duty from Div. School. | |
| -- do -- | 2nd | | | |
| -- do -- | 3rd | | Battn. of 46th Division (5th North Staffords) relieved Battn of 37th Division on our immediate right on night of 3rd/4th | |
| -- do -- | 4th | | 5th South Lancs Regt. relieved us in trenches T. 133 to T. 148. Battn. went into rest huts at GOUY. | |
| -- GOUY | 5th | | Battn. No 2308 Pte 10 nyt W. wounded. G.S.W. chest. | |
| -- do -- | 6th | | Battn. resting at Gouy. | |
| -- do -- | 7th | | Major C.K. Potter rejoined. Divisional School as Commandant | |
| -- do -- | 8th | | Lt. G.S. Watson and Lt. N.G. Richardson attended Gas School at Gouy. Battn. moved to Bellacourt 'A', 'B', 'C' Coys billeted in GROSVILLE 'D' Coy and HdQrs in 2nd debut in BELLACOURT. | |
| BELLACOURT | 9th | | Capt N. Dickinson and C.S.M. Allatoft proceeded to Third Army depot to undergo course of Instruction. Battn. provided 15 officers and 600 men for working parties under R.E. | |
| -- do -- | 10th | | Battn. moved into billets in BRETENCOURT. 2/Lt. C.N. Udall and F.F. Wood joined Battn. from England. Working parties of 15 officers and 600 men again provided for work under R.E. 2/Lt. Kearney and 1 N.C.O. attached M.G. Course at CAMBLIGNEUL | |
| BRETENCOURT | 11th | | No 2893 Pte. Welsh H. 'N Co. G.S.W. head. Battn. provided 15 officers and 600 other ranks for work under R.E. Also 3 Officers 100 other ranks for work under D.O.T.M. No 3525 Pte Banks J. 'A' Co. G.S.W. L. forearm. casualty. | |
| -- do -- | 12th | | Battalion provided further large working parties at night casualties 2308 Pte Boaps W. 'B' Coy, wounded 4th inst, died of wounds. | |
| -- do -- | 13th | | Battn. provided large fatigue parties during night. | |
| -- do -- | 14th | | Battn. provided large fatigue parties during night. 2299 Pte Derbyshire H. 'A' Co. accidentally wounded in hand by explosion of rifle shell. | |
| -- do -- | 15th | | Battn. still providing large working parties. No 1417 Pte Crompton J. 'D' Coy killed in Action | |
| -- do -- | 16th | | Battn. provided large fatigue parties during night. 2/Lt. A. 10. Labourer reported for duty from Base. No 2196 Pte Flanagan attached to 166 Brigade as pigeon flyer. | |

# WAR DIARY
## or
## INTELLIGENCE SUMMARY

Army Form C. 2118

Instructions regarding War Diaries and Intelligence Summaries are contained in F.S. Regs., Part II. and the Staff Manual respectively. Title Pages will be prepared in manuscript.

(Erase heading not required.)

| Place | Date | Hour | Summary of Events and Information | Remarks and references to Appendices |
|---|---|---|---|---|
| BRETENCOURT | 17 July 1916 | | 2/Lt. C. Kenyon, 1542 Sgt. J. Wells and 2544 Cpl. J. Pickering attended Durham School for Course of instruction in Physical Drill and Bayonet fighting. | |
| — do — | 18th | | 3274 Pte. J. Robson proceeded to Base, underage. Battn. proceeded by platoons to GOUY where 3 Coys were billeted in huts and one Coy in village. Details billeted in huts and village. | |
| GOUY | 19th | | Battn. left GOUY at 2.30 pm marching in column of route - Scouts & Gallers, 'C' Coy, 'B' Coy, 'A' Coy, 'D' Coy, Bombers Lewis Gunners. Route FOSSEUX, BARLY, SOMBRIN, LA GRANDE RULLECOURT where we arrived at 5.0 pm and billeted there. | |
| GRANDE RULLECOURT | 20th | | Battn. paraded 6.15 a.m. Order of march Scouts, Signallers, B, A, D, C, Bombers Lewis Gunners. Route SUS. ST- LEGER, IVERGNY, LE BRÉVIÈRES, arriving at billeting place at 8.45 a.m. and billeted there. 17 men fell out on march. Major C.K. Plotter rejoined from Divisional school. | |
| BREVILLERS | 21st | | Battn. paraded 6.50 a.m. in column of route. Order of march. Scouts, Signallers A, D, C, B, Bombers Lewis Gunners. Route - BANQUE MAISON, BARLY, to OUTREBOIS. Battalion night proceeded OUTREBOIS. 2/Lt Jones Cont., Plaster joined Battalion. No. 1405 Pte Matthews W. proceeded to England for Employment in munitions. | |
| OUTREBOIS | 22nd | | Bn. paraded 6.55 am in column of route. Marched via BOIS BERQUES, BERNAVILLE to BEAUMETZ arriving 10 am. Divisional Commander inspected Battalion on the march at BERNAVILLE | |
| BEAUMETZ | 23rd | | No. 2112 Pte. W. Roe proceeded to 166 Trench Mortar Battery for duty. | |
| — do — | 24th | | Battn. proceeded with training. Transports proceeded to Co. S.Y. at 5 a.m. Second line proceeded at 12 noon. | |
| — do — | 25th | | Battn. paraded at 4 p.m. and marched to CANDAS, when we entrained at 11.30 a.m. Strength entraining 41 officers, 885 other ranks. Detrained at MERICOURT, SOMME and marched to billets in VILLE-SUR-ANCRE. 2/Lt. E. Rigby joined Battalion. | |
| VILLE SUR ANCRE | 26th | | 2/Lt. G. Roe reported for duty from Base. | |
| — do — | 27th | | Battn. moved to Bivouac near GUILLEMONT. Offrs. the Cmdg Officers went to recce line which 166th Bde. was to take over facing GUILLEMONT. 2/Lt. W.B. Brooks and 5 men went to 166 T.M. Battery for duty | |
| Nr. MEAULTE | 28th | | No. 5631 Pte. Butler W. proceeded to Etaples - underage. No. 3137 Pte. Ward 'D' Co. proceeded to LE TOQUET M.G. school. 2/Lt. N. Walker interviewed by representative of R.F.C. | |
| — do — | 29th | | No. 5210 Pte. Queegan W. proceeded to ETAPLES - underage. Coy Comdr inspected trenches facing GUILLEMOT | |

**Army Form C. 2118**

# WAR DIARY
## or
## INTELLIGENCE SUMMARY
*(Erase heading not required.)*

Instructions regarding War Diaries and Intelligence Summaries are contained in F. S. Regs., Part II. and the Staff Manual respectively. Title Pages will be prepared in manuscript.

| Place | Date | Hour | Summary of Events and Information | Remarks and references to Appendices |
|---|---|---|---|---|
| N. MEAULTE | 30th July 1916 | | Battn. moved from Bivouac N.E. of MEAULTE to Bivouac F 17 a 5.5 (map. France 62 D NE 1/20000) | |
| | 31st | 4.15 am | Battn. paraded 4.15 a.m. & marched to A 15 a 4.2 (France 62 C. N.W. 1/20000) where Coys. were placed in a portion of the British original front and support lines. Transport remained at CITADEL F 1 a 5.5 (France 62 D N.E. 1/20000) Casualties 7305 Pte Pilling J. C. C. Shell wound – neck. 3630 – Hart J. D. – Shell wound – thigh – at duty | |

M. Ticket
Lieut Col.
Comdg 1/5th Bn. L. N. Lancs. Regt.

166th Brigade.
55th Division

1/5th BATTALION

LOYAL NORTH LANCASHIRE REGIMENT

AUGUST 1916

1/5/ N Lancs
Vol 13
166/55

War Diary
of the
1/5 Loyal North Lanc. R.
for the period
1st August to 31st August
1916.

Army Form C. 2118.

# WAR DIARY
## or
## INTELLIGENCE SUMMARY.
*(Erase heading not required.)*

Instructions regarding War Diaries and Intelligence Summaries are contained in F.S. Regs., Part II. and the Staff Manual respectively. Title pages will be prepared in manuscript.

| Hour, Date, Place | Summary of Events and Information | Remarks and references to Appendices |
|---|---|---|
| 1st August 1916<br>A.15.a.4.2.<br>Sheet62D N-E<br>1/20000<br>France | Battalion still in trenches. Draft of 8 O.R. joined from Base | |
| 2nd August 1916 | Several 8" shells were fired on the trenches in the vicinity of battalion about 8a.m.<br>Casualties.<br>2263 Pte J.Wood Signaller KILLED<br>4143 " J Loftus "D" Co. wounded | |
| 3rd. " | Provided seven parties, each of one officer and 50 other men ranks for carrying, digging, and wiring; but owing to heavy artillery fire during the whole night very little of the work was proceeded with.<br>Casualties.-<br>3717 Pte Lambert G. "C" Coy. wounded - AT DUTY.<br>2504 " Marsh E. "A" CO. " Shell shock. | |
| 4th. " | Still in trenches furnishing working parties.<br>Casualties.<br>14 O.R. wounded. (1 died of wounds 7.8.16. 2 AT DUTY.) | |
| 5th. "<br>6th. " | Still in Reserve trenches providing working parties.<br>Battalion moved into bivouac near Citadel. F.23.a. Sheet 62 D N.E. 1/20,000.France. Capt. P.C.PILLING wounded during heavy shelling of CARNOY Valley, particularly partnear Battn. Hdqtrs. Later died of wounds.<br>Other Casualties.<br>Capt. A.ENTWISLE wounde/d<br>Lieut. and Adjt. W.TONG. " Slight AT DUTY<br>Capt. H.WHITEHEAD " Slight AT DUTY<br>2/Lt. R CROMPTON " Slight AT DUTY.<br>12 O.R. wounded(1 died 6.8.16; 4 AT DUTY. | |
| 7th " <br>F.23.A. | In bivouacs resting | |

(B 29 6) W 4141—463 100,000 9/14 H W V  Forms/C. 2118/10

# WAR DIARY
## or
## INTELLIGENCE SUMMARY.
*(Erase heading not required.)*

Army Form C. 2118.

| Hour, Date, Place | Summary of Events and Information | Remarks and references to Appendices |
|---|---|---|
| A.4.c & d.<br>8th.August 1916 | Battn. moved from bivouac to Dublin trench (A.4.c & d) leaving about 7a.m. Major Potter, Capts. H.Whitehead M.Dickinson, G.M.Hesketh, Lieut. H.A.Richardson, and 2/Lts. Jones,Haslam, Plastow, Rigby, Wood, Green, Lee, Frankland, Udall, Faulkner, and Taberner, and 147 other ranks(specialists) remained behind. About 11p.m. Major Potter received orders to report to Bde. Advanced Hdqtrs.Details were ordered to stand by about midnight,ready to move at a moments notice. (see August 9th.)<br>Casualties.<br>3 other ranks killed. 2 other ranks wounded (1 at duty) | |
| 9th August '16. | The following report on operations contains full details of the action fought on this day :-<br>Report on operations 8th and 9th. August 1916.:-<br>17th. Aug. 1916.- My battalion bivouaced in F23 area. Orders received from 166th. Inf. Bde. ( 166/S/258 ) at 7-51 a.m 8/8/16, to report as Brigade reserve to 164th. Inf Bde. In accordance with instructions received (B.M.540) battalion moved into DUBLIN and CASEMENT trenches, 2 Coys. in each area A.4c and d and A 10, arrived and in position at 9-40 a.m. 8/8/16.- Battalion H.Q. in advance of CASEMENT trench. Instructions received (B6) from 'ROME' to send 2 Coys. to occupy trenches running north between TRONES-GUILLEMONT Rd. and Railway (Support trenches) B and C Coys. moved via MALTZ HORN trench and SUNKEN Rd. S 30 c. An officer detailed by'ROME' acted as guide. Coys. in position at 4 p.m. Subsequently B Coy. was put into front line trench by order of O.C. 8th. Liverpool (Irish) Regt, at 10-10 p.m. 8/8/16 verbal orders received per Staff Captain for C.O. to report to H.Q. 164th. Brigade. On arrival there Operation Orders for attack on by 164th. Brigade were read out. The attack on the morning of the | |

# WAR DIARY
## or
## INTELLIGENCE SUMMARY.
*(Erase heading not required.)*

Army Form C. 2118.

| Hour, Date, Place | Summary of Events and Information | Remarks and references to Appendices |
|---|---|---|
| 9th August 1916<br>A.4.c & d | morning of the 9th. was to be at or not later than 2 am and to be without artillery preparation. 164 Bde. Commander gave orders for remainder of my battalion to move up and occupy trenches at present in occupation by 2/5 Lancs Fusiliers. I pointed out that the report by my Second in command Capt. T. Entwisle that these trenches were greatly over-crowded; 164 Bde. then gave verbal orders that the remaining two companies of my battalion should move into trenches referred to above, which would be vacated by 2/5 Lancs. Fusiliers, which battn. would be out in front of trenches in four waves. At 12.55.a.m. 9th inst. the remaining two companies of my battalion vacated CASEMENT trench and moved into position, reaching the SUNKEN ROAD about 2a.m. Battn H. Qu and Details (Orderlies, HdQtr Signallers and Bombers) remained in Casement Trench. Second in command and Adjt. proceeding with the two companies.<br>Operation Orders 17 of 166 Bde. were received at 2.30 a.m. on 9th, inst. at SUNKENROAD – also received at this time wire No. 15 from Brigadier 166 Inf. Bde– B.M. 11 from "ROME" –and notification that zero hour would be at 4.20a.m. The operation timed for 2a.m. by 164 Bde. had not taken place and subsequently it was ascertained that this operation had been postponed to 4.15.a.m. or five minutes before the task allotted to my battalion was due to commence.<br>Re para 5 Operation Order 17 of 166 Bde. the trees trenches therein referred to viz., EDWARDS & FAGIN could not be located, nor could 2/5 Lancs Fusiliers supply any information or planes to situation of same. Owing to this lack of information the order re occupying these trenches could not be carried out. The dispositions of companies of my battalion at this time being as under :- | |

# WAR DIARY
## or
## INTELLIGENCE SUMMARY.

*(Erase heading not required.)*

Army Form C. 2118.

| Hour, Date, Place | Summary of Events and Information | Remarks and references to Appendices |
|---|---|---|
| 9th. Aug. 1916. cd. A 4 c & d. | Front Line- TRONES WOOD-GUILLEMONT RD. to RAILWAY---1 Coy In trench about 200 yds. behind above ---1 Coy. In SUNKEN ROAD --- 2 Coys. An Officer was despatched to the 1/10th. Liverpool(Scottish) Regiment to get in touch and returned with report that they were going to attack as per O.O. 17 . (This Officer returned after the German barrage had commenced). An effort to get in touch with 2nd. Division failed. Position of B & C Coys in front line was not at this time known to Battalion H.Q. Owing to the difficulty stated above the operation was only carried out with 2 Coys, and a portion of the third. Owing to pressure of time all attempts at written orders were now abandoned and verbal instructions were issued by Capt. T. Entwisle to each of three Coy. Cmdrs. in assembly trenches,(the position of B Coy. in front trench having by this time been ascertained). Orders issued were:- Battalion will attack in 4 waves conjunctly with Liverpool Scottish on right and 2nd. Division on left. Objective-- 1.Enemy front line. 2. Capture of GUILLEMONT. Time--- ---Watch Liverpool Scottish on right and advance in, waves with them. Battalion H.Q. will be that of 2/5th. Lancashire Fusiliers. D Coy. detailed to attack with right flank on TRONES→ GUILLEMONT ROAD A Coy. detailed to clear an old quarry. B Coy. to attack on left of A Coy. with left flank resting on RAILWAY. C Coy. (position of this Coy. was not located until about 7 a.m. in trenches East of TRONES WOOD. Owing to complicatd nature of trenches, the assembly being fed by one narrow C.T. which was very much congested | |

# WAR DIARY
## or
## INTELLIGENCE SUMMARY.
(Erase heading not required.)

Army Form C. 2118.

| Hour, Date, Place | Summary of Events and Information | Remarks and references to Appendices |
|---|---|---|
| 9th. August 1916 A.4.c&d | congested there being in the same area parties of 2/5 Lancs Fusiliers and other units waiting for order to attack, the Coy. detailed for QUARRY was late in getting up. It became subsequently that some parties 2/5 Lancs. Fusiliers went overwith our two Coys. Preparations for the attack commenced at 5.10a.m and attack was launched aat 5.25 a.m. From the outset very heavy machine gun firewas encountered on our right; Left Coy progressed well getting within 250 yards of German line, but seeing the right held up and all officers except one being casualties, survivors of this company took, cover in shell holes.Meanwhile the right company having lost toych with left company and parties of LiverpoolScottish returning to original line, report was sent to me that men were digging in 30 yards in advance of original line, upon receipt of which message I ordered withdrawal to original line, further advance being impracticable. Instructions received by me on being ordered up were that my battalion was to be in reserve to 164 Bde. and establish my Hdqtrs. in CASEMENT trench . No orders to the contrary were received at any time. On remaining 2 Coys being ordered up undered up under command of Capt. T. Entwisle I instructed him to report when in position and where Battn. Hdqtrs. were established. This report was received by me at 4a.m. at Casement Trench when I at once proceeded with Hdqtr. details arriving in SUNKEN ROAD when two Coys. had been launched to the attack. Until arrival at SUNKEN ROAD Ihad not seen O.O.17 the position of my Hdqtrs. at CASEMENT trench had been reporte d to 164 & 166 Inf. Bdes.<br><br>(Sd) G.Hesketh,Lt Col<br>11.8.16   Cmdg. 1/5 Loyal N.Lancs. Regiment.<br>The following was sent in continuance of the foregoing some days later but it contains some bearing on the events about this period;— | |

Army Form C. 2118.

# WAR DIARY
## or
## INTELLIGENCE SUMMARY.

(Erase heading not required.)

Instructions regarding War Diaries and Intelligence Summaries are contained in F.S. Regs., Part II. and the Staff Manual respectively. Title pages will be prepared in manuscript.

| Hour, Date, Place | Summary of Events and Information | Remarks and references to Appendices |
|---|---|---|
| 9th. Aug 1916 <br> A 4 c.& d. | At 10-45 a.m. 9/8/16 received intimation from Brigade that Battalion would be relieved immediately by 1/5th. South Lan. Regt. Relief was carried out later, the whole battalion withdrawing to DUBLIN and CASEMENT trenches; relief completed 3-15 p.m. Reinforcement, (Details left behind at Transport field) reported at 8-30 p.m. During the night of the 9/10th. several parties were supplied to the left sector for clearing battlefield and improving trenches. <br> In accordance with O.O.78 received at 6-46 p.m. 10/8/16 my battalion vacated DUBLIN and CASEMENT trenches and moved into bivouac in area F 22 c & d arriving about 10-30 pm. In the meantime a proposed operation in accordance with instructions received verbally from the G.O.C. late in the afternoon of the 10th., subsequently amplified by wire No. 18 of 166th. Brigade, was, after all the necessary orders and preparations being made, and ground reconnoitred by Officers selected, cancelled. During the 11th. battalion completed with picks and spades and bombs. <br> At 3 pm. on the 11th. inst. warning was received to be in readiness to move at short notice (B.M. 600).at 10-30 pm. received orders to proceed to Divisional Headquartersat 1 am. 12th. inst. to meet guide from 165th. Bde. who would lead battalion into Dublin and Casement trenches, where I was to come under the orders of 165th. Bde. <br> About 11 pm. above order was cancelled but received intimation to be in readiness to move at short notice. <br> 12th. inst. spent in refitting and cleaning up. <br> 13th inst. Practiced the attack in conjunction with 5th. King's Own (R.L.) Regt. on model trenches representing a portion of the enemy's trenches south of GUILLEMONT. <br> About 9pm. received orders to move down as soon as possible into old British front line trenches near TALUS BOISE A 9 c & d. Arrived about 11-55 pm. <br> 14th. Spent in supplying working parties. At 7-30 pm. on | |

Army Form C. 2118.

# WAR DIARY
## or
## INTELLIGENCE SUMMARY.
*(Erase heading not required.)*

Instructions regarding War Diaries and Intelligence Summaries are contained in F.S. Regs., Part II. and the Staff Manual respectively. Title pages will be prepared in manuscript.

| Hour, Date, Place | Summary of Events and Information | Remarks and references to Appendices |
|---|---|---|
| 9th Aug. 1916<br>A 4 c&d | arrival of a brigade of the 24th Div. the battn. commenced to withdraw reaching bivouac F.22.C & D 9.40p.m. On afternoon of 15th Battn moved via. Citadel, Sandpit, Carcaillot Farm, to MEAULTE, arriving at billets there at 5.0 p.m. On 16th G.O.C. 55th Div. inspected the battalion. On 17th Reinforcements, 94 O.R. reported for duty(All from 5th E. Lanc Rgt.) On 19th Battn moved by train from EDGE HILL siding to MARTAINVILLE detraining about 6.55p.m. Marched to ACHEUX. Batt'n. reported in billets at m10p.m. (Sd) G.Hesketh, Lt Col<br><br>22.8.16  Cmdg. 1/5 Loyal N. LANcs Rgt.<br>The following officers took part in the action of August 9 16<br>Lt. Col G.Hesketh<br>Major C.K.Potter (Advanced Bde. HdQtrs)<br>Capt T Entwisle. (wounded)<br>Lieut. G.S.Watson<br>"  F.K.Mallet<br>"  H. Chronnell A/Adjt.<br>"  R.K.Makeant<br>"  Ernest Blackburn (Killed)<br>2/" Edward Blackburn (Killed)<br>"  A.Kenyon<br>"  C Marshall<br>"N.Walker  (Bde. H.Q.)<br>Lieut E.H Ward  (wounded)<br>2/" S.L.Redfern<br>"  J.J.Crabtree<br>"  R.Crompton<br>"  B.Kearney<br>E.W.Rice  (Killed )<br>"  C.B.Coldham  (Bde H.Q.)<br>"  S.J.Curtis  (killed)<br>"  J.Farnworth<br>"  E.Harling<br>Capt.N.J.Giblin Med.Off.R.A.M.C. | |

Army Form C. 2118.

# WAR DIARY
## or
## INTELLIGENCE SUMMARY.
*(Erase heading not required.)*
(8)

Instructions regarding War Diaries and Intelligence Summaries are contained in F.S. Regs., Part II. and the Staff Manual respectively. Title pages will be prepared in manuscript.

| Hour, Date, Place | Summary of Events and Information | Remarks and references to Appendices |
|---|---|---|
| 9.8.16 | Casualties (For officer casualties see previous page). 26 O.R. Killed in action. 86 O.R. Wounded (3 since died of wounds; 7 AT DUTY) 20 O.R. Missing (1 rejoined; 5 since reported wounded in hospital) | |
| 10.8.16 F.22.c.& d | Battn. remained in DUBLIN *trenches*. Germans shelled trench fairly heavily during day evidently endeavouring to locate batteries At 9.45.p.m. Battn proceeded to vacate trenches and marched by platoons at 200 yards interval to bivouac F.22.c. & d. Casualties 2564 Cpl Norburn F. ) wounded AT DUTY 2043 R.Q.M.S. Herbert H. ) 3148 Pte O'Toole J. accidentally wounded. | |
| 11.8.16 | Battn. still in bivouac. No 4442 Pte Parsons J. proceeded to 4th. Army Lewis Gun School. Battn ordered to "Stand to" about 4p.m.. Later orders received for every man to have 2 bombs and 3 sandbags. Orders to "Stand to" cancelled about 11p.m. | |
| 12.8.16 | Battn. remained in bivouac resting. | |
| 13.8.16 | Battn. practised attack in conjunction with 5th King's Own (R.L.) Rgt. on model trenches. 2/Lt. Udell and 3 O.R. proceeded to 4th Army Telescopic Sight School. Battn took over trenches in old British front line. Order received 9p.m.. In Position 11p.m. | |
| 14.8.16 | Battn provided various digging and burying parties. No 2535 Pte R.S.Mowle proceeded to 4th Army Trench Mortar School Battn. relieved in trenches and marched to bivouacs F.22.c.&d | |

Army Form C. 2118.

# WAR DIARY
## or
## INTELLIGENCE SUMMARY.
(Erase heading not required.)

Instructions regarding War Diaries and Intelligence Summaries are contained in F. S. Regs., Part II. and the Staff Manual respectively. Title pages will be prepared in manuscript.

| Hour, Date, Place | Summary of Events and Information | Remarks and references to Appendices |
|---|---|---|
| 14.8.16<br>F22.c & d<br>15.8.16 | Casualties.<br>60.R. wounded (1 since died of wounds; 1 AT DUTY)<br>At 3p.m. Battn moved via CITADEL, SANDPIT, Cailcallot Farm to Meaulte where we went into billets | |
| 16.8.16 | Div. Cmdr. General Jeudwin C.B. inspected Battn on parade at 5p.m. in field S.W. of VIVIER MILL MEAULTE<br>Casualty.<br>1687 Pte Jolly H. accidentally wounded | |
| 17.8.16 | Draft of 94 O.R. joined Battn from 25th, INF Base. All belonged to 1/5 E.Lancs. Rgt, and many had seen active service in Gallipoli. Their physical standard appeared to be about the average. The draft was allotted as under :-<br>"B" Coy. 55 including 1 subst. C.S.M.<br>"C" " 10 " 1 " Sgt.<br>"D" " 29 " 1 paid L/Sgt | |
| 18.8.16 | Still at Meaulte. Battn. carried on with training. C.O. inspected draft at 2p.m. | |
| 19.8.16 | Battn entrained at EDGE/ Hill Siding South of ALBERT.. Departed at 2p.m. and detrained at MARTAINVILLE at about 6.55pm Marched to ACHEUX where we went into billets arriving 10pm | |
| 20.8.;6<br>ACHEUX | Battn rested. No 4267 Pte J.Hunt went for course to 4th Army Lewis Gun School, Le Touquet Golf links, ETAPLES. Draft of 25 O.R. joined Battn. from Base Etaples. 4 O.R. E.Lancs ditto. | |
| 21.8.16 | 2/Lts Crompton and Curtis with 26 O.R. of "A" Co. proceeded to the seaside at AULT on 3 days leave. | |
| 22.8.16 | Maj.Gen. Jeudwine C.B. addressed 50% officers and N.C.O's at Chepy. | |

Army Form C. 2118.

# WAR DIARY
## or
## INTELLIGENCE SUMMARY.
(Erase heading not required.)

Instructions regarding War Diaries and Intelligence
Summaries are contained in F.S. Regs., Part II.
and the Staff Manual respectively. Title pages
will be prepared in manuscript.

| Hour, Date, Place | Summary of Events and Information | Remarks and references to Appendices |
|---|---|---|
| 23.8.16 Acheux | Lt. Col. G.Hesketh D.S.O. performed the duties of Brigadier temporarily during absence of Briig.Gen. L.Green Wilkinson, Cmdg. 166 Bde.. Battn. granted half holiday inafternoon,and passes to Abbeville not exceeding 10% per Coy granted. No.1631 Cpl Connor J. and 6 men reported to C.R.E. 55th Div. for employment with 55 Div. Tunneling Co. Casualties. 6917 Pte Wharmby A. ) accidentally wounded AT DUTY. 3258 " Pilkington J ) | |
| 24.8.16 | Second party of 2 Officers(2/Lts Marshell and Crabtree) 28 O.R from "B" Coy. granted 3 days leave at the seaside at AULT. Draft of 9 O.R. joined Battn from Base ETAPLES. Casualty. 19069 Pte Watkinson G. 7th L.N.L. att'D found dead in billet. Finding of COurt of Enquiry- Death from natural causes. | |
| 25.8.16 | Still in Acheux continuing training | |
| 26.8.16 | 3rd party - Details- 1 officer(2/lt.N.Walker) and 19 O.R. granted 3 days to Ault. C.S.M. Hodgkiss attached to Battn for one day for purpose of giving instruction in Bayonet fighting. Casualty; 2182 Pte R.Roscoe wounded accidentally. | |
| 27.8 16 | Received warning Order for Transport to be prepared to move to new area by noon 28th. All further leave in France cancelled by Bde. Draft of 24 O.R. 24 O.R. from 1/4 L.N.L. | |
| 28.8.16 | All mounted portions of Transport proceeded to TRANSLOY at 3.30 P.M. Draft of 5 O.R. joined Battn. from 1/4l.N.L. | |
| 29.8.16 | Draft of 26 O.R. joined Battn from Base Depot Etaples. Warning Order received at 12 noon for Battn to be prepared to move at very short notice. Later on 4. eve- orders received 12.50p.m. for Battn. to move at 5p.m. via Touffles to BEHEN.Arrived BEHEN 4.40p.m. Very heavy rainstorm during march. | |
| 30 8.16 | Battn paraded ay 2.50a.m. and marched off at 3.0 a.m. for PONT REMY.Arrived 6.30 a.m. and entrained at 7a.m. Strength | |

Army Form C. 2118.

# WAR DIARY
## or
## INTELLIGENCE SUMMARY.
(*Erase heading not required.*)

Instructions regarding War Diaries and Intelligence
Summaries are contained in F. S. Regs., Part II.
and the Staff Manual respectively. Title pages
will be prepared in manuscript.

| Hour, Date, Place | Summary of Events and Information | Remarks and references to Appendices |
|---|---|---|
| 30th Aug. 1916. | Strength entraining 28 Officers 320 other ranks. Detrained at Mericourt 11-10 a.m. and marched to bivouac in cornfield (E7 Sheet 62D n.e.) Heavy rain during whole of day and night. Troops constructed bivouacs with sheaves of corn. Ground in wretchedly soaked and muddy condition. Divisional Commander visited us during day. | |
| 31st. Aug. 1916. | Weather brighter and drier. Moved at 1-30 p.m. after re-stacking corn, to new bivouac E 12 A.. Orders issued to be prepared to move at short notice in fighting order. 6 officers, as under, joined battalion from England:- 2nd. Lieut. G. Glaister. 2nd. Lieut. W. Ingham.     "     W.A. Arthur.     "     T.S. Morris.     "     C.B. Wray.     "     G.E. Riding. | |

Lieut. Colonel,
for Cmdg. 1/5th. Bn. Lo al N. Lancs. Regt.

166/55
Vol 14

War Diary
of
1/5th N. Lancs. R.

1st September to 30th September 1916

Army Form C. 2118

# WAR DIARY
## or
## INTELLIGENCE SUMMARY

1/5th. Loyal N. Lancs. Regt.

(Erase heading not required.)

Instructions regarding War Diaries and Intelligence Summaries are contained in F.S. Regs., Part II. and the Staff Manual respectively. Title Pages will be prepared in manuscript.

| Place | Date | Hour | Summary of Events and Information | Remarks and references to Appendices |
|---|---|---|---|---|
| Area E 12 a Sheet 57d NE | 1/Sept.'16. | | Battalion still in bivouac. Coy Cmdrs. visited trenches, in front of Delville Wood during afternoon so as to become acquainted with the lie of the land, etc. Major C.K. Potter left battalion to take over command of 1/7th. Bn. King's Liverpool Regt. Orders issued re taking over trenches from 9th. Royal West Kent Rgt. on 2nd. inst. | |
| | 2 Sept.'16. | | Lt. H.A. Richardson and 20 orderlies went to H.Q. of 72nd. Infty. Bde. at Quarry at 7 a.m. Warning order notice increased to 4 hrs. In evening battalion practised taking over and handing over of trenches also posting of sentries. Draft of 23 other ranks (22 of 1/5th. East Lancs. Rgt.) reported for duty from Base depot ETAPLES. | |
| | 3 Sept.'16. | | Still in bivouac. Orders received 8-30 p.m. to be ready to move at one hours notice. | |
| | 4 Sept. 1916. | | Orders issued 1 a.m. for battalion to proceed to take over trenches in front of Delville Wood. Orders were cancelled at 8-30a.m. | |
| | 5 Sept.'16. | | Battalion left bivouac at 5 p.m. to relieve the 9th.(S) Bn. East Surrey Regt. in trenches in front of Delville Wood. Marched in column of route to Montauban where battalion split up into platoons. Relief completed 4 a.m. 6/9/16. 1st. Division on our left, 7th. Division on our right. Disposition of battalion:- Front line, C&D Coys. Folly & York trench- A & B Coys. Front line was too crowded, consequently one platoon from each of C & D Coys. were withdrawn to York Trench. Lt. and Adjt. W. Tong rejoined from England. | |
| | 6 Sept.'16. | | Salvage and burying parties busy whole day. Front line very quiet; area about Bn. H.Q. shelled intermittently by heavies. No damage. Division on our right (7th.) launched attack on Ginchy in early afternoon; it did not succeed. Casualties --- Wounded, 2/Lt. T.S. Morris. " E. Rigby. | |

1875 Wt. W593/826 1,000,000 4/15 J.B.C. & A. A.D.S.S./Forms/C. 2118.

Army Form C. 2118

1/5 Loyal N Lancs, R.

(2)

# WAR DIARY
or
## INTELLIGENCE SUMMARY
*(Erase heading not required.)*

Instructions regarding War Diaries and Intelligence Summaries are contained in F. S. Regs., Part II. and the Staff Manual respectively. Title Pages will be prepared in manuscript.

| Place | Date | Hour | Summary of Events and Information | Remarks and references to Appendices |
|---|---|---|---|---|
| Trenches N.E. Edge DELVILLE WD. | 6.9.16(Cntd) 7.9.16 | | Casualties . Other ranks (cont) Killed 4 Wounded 38 (1 at duty) Salvage and burying parties continued work throughout the day. Whole night spent in consolidating front held; a good substantial trench was completed all along Battn. front while the 1/5 S.Lancs R. and L'Pool Scottish constructed and manned strong points in advance of front line. Casualties. Officer. Wounded 2/Lt E. Harling. O.R. Killed 6 Wounded 30 (6 at duty) | |
| | 8.9.16 | | Continued salvaging burying; and consolidating line Casualties. O.R. Killed 1 Wounded 10 (1 died of wounds) (1 at duty) | |
| | 9.9.16 | | Battn. relieved in front line by 1/5 Bn. South Lancs Rgt; We occupied CHECK LINE. Germans fired gas-shells into line between 2.30 and 4p.m. Instructed by Brigade to send up one coy. and two squads of bombers to be under the orders of O.C.1/5 South Lancs Rgt. "A" Coy detailed and marched up, at 9.45.p.m. "A" Coy ordered to hold FOLLY TRENCH and bombers to hold BLOCK at junction of HOP ALLEY and front line. Our artillery opened heavy fire on German positions about 4.30 p.m. Bombardment lasted throughout day and night. Casualties. O.R. Killed 3 Wounded 11 (3 at duty) | |
| | 10.9.16 | | "A" Coy and bombers remained under orders of 1/5 South Lancs RGT. Remainder of Battn. still in CHECK LINE. Casualties: Officers. Wounded 2/Lt. J.S. Curtis O.R. Killed 2 Wounded 9 (2at duty). | |

1875 Wt. W593/826 1,000,000 4/15 J.B.C. & A. A.D.S.S./Forms/C. 2118.

Army Form C. 2118

Instructions regarding War Diaries and Intelligence Summaries are contained in F.S. Regs, Part II. and the Staff Manual respectively. Title Pages will be prepared in manuscript.

# 1/5th. Bn. Loyal N. Lancs. Regt.

## WAR DIARY
or
## INTELLIGENCE SUMMARY
*(Erase heading not required.)*

| Place | Date | Hour | Summary of Events and Information | Remarks and references to Appendices |
|---|---|---|---|---|
| Trenches. | 11 Sept. '16. | | Battalion (less A Coy and 2 squads Bombers under orders of 1/5th. South Lancs. Regt.) moved from CHECK line to Transport at FRICOURT and after a short rest continued march to bivouac area B 12 D (62dNE) arriving 5 p.m. Casualties, Other ranks, Wounded 7 (1 at duty) | |
| | 12 Sept '16 | | Battalion rested. A Coy and 2 squads Bombers still attached to 1/5th South Lancs. Regt. Casualties, Other ranks, Killed One. Wounded Three. | |
| | 13 Sept '16 | | A Coy and 2 squads Bombers rejoined battalion at 11 a.m. Battalion carried on Training during day. | |
| | 14 Sept '16 | | Still in bivouacs. | |
| | 15 Sept '16 | | 3306 Pte T. Makin and 4044 Pte Hargreaves (1/5th. East Lancs. Reg⟨t⟩) proceeded to No. 17 Ordnance Workshop HEILLY, for duty as fitters. News received of successful operations on the British front--- Capture of FLERS? MARTINPUICH? and COURCELLETTE. | |
| | 16 Sept '16 | | Battalion moved to new bivouac 1 mile S.E. of ALBERT. Bivouac shells about 5 p.m. Casualties, Other ranks, Wounded One. | |
| | 17 Sept '16. | | The C.O. and Coy. Cmdrs. visited the line held by 41st. Div. in front of FLERS. Party left bivouac about 1 a.m. Battalion left bivouac at 1-15 p.m. and moved to area of POMMIER REDOUBT, S side of MAMETZ)MONTAUBAN Rd. where instructions were awaited re taking over of trenches from 41st. Div. 1390 Pte Fielding R, A Coy. ⟩ To 15th. Corps. Lewis Gun Course. 2510 " Matthews M, B " ⟩ To 15th. Corps. Trench Mortar Course. 8605 " Crowther F,C " ⟩ Army of 30. o.R.(5 Lewis) Reported for duty 8605 " Crowther F,C " ⟩ | |
| | 18 Sept '16 | | Battalion moved into Reserve trenches about 800 yds. N.E. of Delville Wood relieving 1/7th. King's Liverpool Regt. and in evening moved to trenches at cross-roads N.E. of FLERS. (N 31 b 6.0 ) Two German prisoners taken about 8-30 p.m. by 'C' Coy. Transport and Quartermasters Stores moved to bivouac near POMMIER REDOUBT between MAMETZ and MONTAUBAN on N. side of road. / Casualties, Other ranks, Wounded, One. | |

1875 Wt. W593/826 1,000,000 4/15 J.B.C. & A. A.D.S.S./Forms/C. 2118.

Army Form C. 2118

1/5 Loyal N Lancs Rgt.

# WAR DIARY
or
INTELLIGENCE SUMMARY

(Erase heading not required.)

| Place | Date | Hour | Summary of Events and Information | Remarks and references to Appendices |
|---|---|---|---|---|
| | 19.9.16 (cont) N.31.b.6.0. (57 CS.W.) | | Commenced digging strong points in front of trenches. Burying parties also employed. Men suffered much from cold and wet weather about this period. Casualties. O.R. Killed 2 Wounded 8 | |
| | 20.9.16 | | Continued strong points. During day our heavies dropped several rounds short, but luckily caused no casualties. Casualties. O.R. Killed 1 Wounded 5 | |
| | 21.9.16 | | Continued digging strong points during points --night Casualties. O.R. Killed 1 Wounded 5 (1 at duty). | |
| | 22.9.16 | | Continued digging strong points during night. Our heavy artillery set fire during the afternoon to what appeared to be enemy ammunition dumps, one in the area of SEVEN DIALS and the other about LIGNY - THILLOY. Casualties Officers. Wounded. Lt. H.A.Richardson. O.R. Killed 1 Wounded 10. (3 at duty) | |
| | 23.9.16 | | Battn. relieved during night of 23/24th by a unit of the 165 Bde., and moved to bivouac in area POMMIER REDOUBT on south side of MAMETZ - MONTAUBAN ROAD. Casualties. O.R. Wounded 1 | |
| | 24.9.16 25.9.16 26.9.16 27.9.16 | | Battn. rested in bivouac. Battn carried on training. Still in bivouacs; carried on training. Provided working parties each of one officer and 100 O.R. first from 7a.m. to 1p.m. and second from 1p.m. to 7p.m. repairing LONGUEVAL - FLERS ROAD. German aeroplanes dropped bombs on our transport lines and neighbouring bivouacs about midnight, causing some casualties chiefly to horses | |

Army Form C. 2118

Instructions regarding War Diaries and Intelligence Summaries are contained in F.S. Regs., Part II. and the Staff Manual respectively. Title Pages will be prepared in manuscript.

# 1/5 Loyal N.Lancs.Rgt.
# WAR DIARY
or
# INTELLIGENCE SUMMARY
(Erase heading not required.)

| Place | Date | Hour | (5) Summary of Events and Information | Remarks and references to Appendices |
|---|---|---|---|---|
| Bivouac POMMIER REDOUBT | 27.9.16 (cont) | | Casualties. O.R.   Killed   4<br>                      Wounded  1 | |
| | 28.9.16 | | Marched from bivouac to RIBEMONT via FRICOURT BECORDEL MEAULTE DERNANCOURT & DUIRE. arriving at about 4.30 p.m. two companies in billets and two in bivouac. | |
| | 29.9.16 | | Rested in RIBEMONT | |
| | 30.9.16 | | Battn. paraded in Main street 12.20p.m. and marched to EDGE HILL and there entrained at 2p.m. Detrained at LONGPRE at 1a.m. the f following day, and marched to billets at EAUCOURT | |

                                                   Captain.
                                  Cmdg. 1/5 Loyal N. Lancashire Regt.

Vol 15

War Diary.
of
1/5th N. Lan. Regt
for the period
1st to 31st October 1916

CONFIDENTIAL

Army Form C. 2118.

# WAR DIARY
## or
## INTELLIGENCE SUMMARY.
*(Erase heading not required.)*

Instructions regarding War Diaries and Intelligence Summaries are contained in F. S. Regs., Part II. and the Staff Manual respectively. Title pages will be prepared in manuscript.

| Place | Date | Hour | Summary of Events and Information | Remarks and references to Appendices |
|---|---|---|---|---|
| BAUCOURT, SOMME. | 1st October, 1916. | | Arrived in billets at Baucourt, Somme, 4 a.m., and rested day. | |
| | 2nd October, 1916. | | Paraded in Baucourt, 11-15 a.m. and marched circuitously to ABBEVILLE, where we entrained at 2 p.m. Distance of march; 12 Kilos. Left ABBEVILLE about 3-30 p.m. Detrained at PROVEN BELGIUM following morning. Party of 1 Officer (2 Lt. Kearney) and 100 other ranks remained behind at ABBEVILLE loading wagons. | |
| PROVEN, BELGIUM. | 3rd October, 1916. | | Detrained at PROVEN at 5 a.m. and marched to war hutments camp. Rested remainder of day. Draft of 1 Officer, (2 Lt. J.S. Carr) and 9 other ranks joined Battn. from Base. Rear Party joined from ABBEVILLE. | |
| | 4th October, 1916. | | Left hutments at 3-45 p.m., and marched to siding N. of POPERINGHE where we entrained for YPRES. Detrained at YPRES, 7 p.m. and met guides from Liverpool Scottish and 1/14 South Wales Borderers, who conducted Battalion to Reserve line on YSER CANAL. | |
| | 5th October, 1916. | | | |
| | 6th October, 1916. | | No. 4092, Private J. Pickvance to Base, under age. "A" Coy. furnished one platoon to hold LA BRIQUE POST (c26d 60.10) map ST. JULIEN, 28 N.W.2. Furnished Working party for Front line. Officers leave reopened. Lt. Chronnell proceeded on leave first. | |

# WARR DIARY
## or
## INTELLIGENCE SUMMARY.
*(Erase heading not required.)*

Army Form C. 2118.

Instructions regarding War Diaries and Intelligence Summaries are contained in F. S. Regs., Part II. and the Staff Manual respectively. Title pages will be prepared in manuscript.

| Place | Date | Hour | Summary of Events and Information | Remarks and references to Appendices |
|---|---|---|---|---|
| TRENCHES, YPRES. | 7th October, 1916. | | Sgt. Melia, J. "D" Coy. <br> Cpl. Leigh, W. "C" Coy. } To 4th Army Gas School, CASSELL. <br> " Anderson, J. "A" Coy. } <br> " Pickering, G. "B" Coy. } <br> Furnished working parties for Front and Support lines at night. | |
| | 8th October, 1916. | | Following N.C.O's. and men proceeded to VIII Corps, Senior Officers' Training School:- <br> 2376 Private A. Turnbull  3461 Private W. Crompton <br> 7740   "   W. Johnson    8653    "    R.J.Wearne <br> 3957 L/Cpl. J. Carroll    3266 L/Cpl. H. Standish <br> 2442 Private F. Waller   2481 Private W. Brown <br> 3312    "    W. Grimshaw <br> Furnished working parties for Front and Rear lines during night. | |
| | 9th October, 1916. | | Battalion issued with 1 box respirator per officer and man. Provided working parties on Front and Rear lines during night, also party employed organising and constructing Battalion Dump. | |
| | 10th October, 1916. | | Provided working parties as for previous day. | |
| | 11th October, 1916. | | Provided working parties as for 9th October, and additional party - under Signal Officer - of 50 other ranks. | |
| | 12th October, 1916. | | Parties provided as for previous nights for work on Front and Support lines. | |

Army Form C. 2118.

# WAR DIARY
## or
## INTELLIGENCE SUMMARY.
(Erase heading not required.)

Instructions regarding War Diaries and Intelligence
Summaries are contained in F. S. Regs., Part II.
and the Staff Manual respectively. Title pages
will be prepared in manuscript.

| Place | Date | Hour | Summary of Events and Information | Remarks and references to Appendices |
|---|---|---|---|---|
| | 13th October, 1916. | | Relieved Liverpool Scottish Regiment in front line system of trenches (C.) 9 (a. 70.10 to C.14.k.15.15). Rif map. SECRET wt.19 Companies allotted as follows:- <br> "C" Company in front line - RIGHT subsector. <br> "D" " " " - LEFT " <br> "B" " support line. <br> "A" " reserve in ST. JEAN. <br> Relief completed 9-30 p.m. <br> Enemy showed no activities during relief. <br> On our right:- 1/5th Battalion Kings Own (R.L.) Regt. <br> On our left:- 14th Battalion S. Wales Borders. (38 Div.) | |
| | 14th October, 1916 | | Front line, right subsector minen-werfered during morning between 10 a.m. and 1 p.m. <br> Casualties:- Other Ranks, wounded 3 (2 slight at duty). | |
| | 15th October, 1916. | | Draft of 15 Other Ranks joined Battalion from Base. <br> "C" Company were shelled with minen-werfers during morning, and parapet badly damaged in places. Our Artillery retaliation appeared to be ineffective. <br> Battalion on our right, 5th Kings Own (R.L.) Regt. conducted a raid on German trenches opposite their sector. | |
| | 16th October, 1916. | | 2/Lieut. C.B.Wray and 3 other ranks proceeded to IMTOUQUET School for Lewis Gun Course. <br> Enemy minen-werfers again active on our front. Part of JOHN STREET knocked down. As previously, our Artillery retaliation seemed ineffective. | |
| | 17th October, 1916. | | Casualties:- <br> 1785 Private Wilson, E. "D" Company wounded, slight, at duty. | |

Army Form C. 2118.

# WAR DIARY
## or
## INTELLIGENCE SUMMARY.
*(Erase heading not required.)*

Instructions regarding War Diaries and Intelligence Summaries are contained in F. S. Regs., Part II. and the Staff Manual respectively. Title pages will be prepared in manuscript.

| Place | Date | Hour | Summary of Events and Information | Remarks and references to Appendices |
|---|---|---|---|---|
| TRENCHES, YPRES. | 18th October, 1916. | | "A" and "B" Companies relieved "C" and "D" Companies respectively. About 9 p.m. Germans opened heavy bombardment by trench mortars and field guns on RIGHT subsector, held by "A" Company, and the trenches immediately on right and left of this point. JOHN STREET was also shelled. These trenches were crowded at this time and many casualties (approximately 50) resulted in consequence. A party of Liverpool Scottish were passing along the trench carrying material, and another party were engaged working in front of the parapet when the shelling commenced. The bombardment lasted 40 minutes, and enemy machine guns fired on various points throughout this period. When the bombardment ceased, all available men were busily engaged cleaning up, for the damage both to front line trench and JOHN STREET was great.<br>Casualties:- Other ranks. Killed 5. Wounded 19 including one died of wounds, and two slight at duty. | |
| | 19th October, 1916. | | Nil. | |
| | 20th October, 1916. | | Draft of 11 Officers joined Battalion from Base for duty. These Officers belong to the following Regiments:-<br>4 to 8th Manchester Regiment. ½<br>1 to 9th "<br>6 to 4th Royal Welsh Fusiliers. | |
| | 23rd October, 1916. | | Battalion relieved by 1/8th Battalion Liverpool (Irish) Regt. Relief completed 9-30 p.m. On relief Companies marched to entraining point near Asylum, Ypres, and there | |

2353 Wt. W2544/1454 700,000 5/15 D. D. & L. A.D.S.S./Forms/C. 2118.

Army Form C. 2118.

# WAR DIARY
## or
## INTELLIGENCE SUMMARY.

(Erase heading not required.)

Instructions regarding War Diaries and Intelligence
Summaries are contained in F. S. Regs., Part II.
and the Staff Manual respectively. Title pages
will be prepared in manuscript.

| Place | Date | Hour | Summary of Events and Information | Remarks and references to Appendices |
|---|---|---|---|---|
| | 23rd October, 1916. (continued) | | entrained. Detrained at B Camp (BRANDHOEK) about midnight. Casualties:- Other ranks, wounded 3, including 3314 Private F. Greenhalgh, self-inflicted. | |
| | 24th October, 1916. | | Provided 1 Officer and 200 men for work on cable trench in H.4.a.Central. Remainder of men occupied in cleaning up. | |
| | 25th October, 1916. | | Still in B Camp. | |
| | 26th October, 1916. | | Again provided party of one Officer and 200 men digging cable trench. | |
| | 30th October, 1916. | | Entrained at B Camp, 5 p.m. Detrained at YPRES 6 p.m. Relieved 1/8th Liverpool (Irish) Regt. in reserve line on YSER CANAL bank. Relief completed 8 p.m. 2/Lieut. Barrett and Corporal Curtiss proceeded to TERDEGHEM for course of Grenade instruction, and Lance Corporal Croft, "B" Company for Trench Mortar course. | |
| | 31st October, 1916. | | Battalion moved from CANAL bank to relieve 2/5th Lancashire Fusiliers in front line system, left Brigade Sector. "C" Company took over LEFT subsector. "D" Company " " RIGHT subsector. "A" Company " " SUPPORT line "B" Company in reserve in ST. JEAN. Relief completed about 9 p.m. Liverpool Scottish took over from us on CANAL bank. | |

2353  Wt. W2541/1454 700,000 5/15 D. D. & L.   A.D.S.S./Forms/C. 2118.

CONFIDENTIAL

Vol 16

War Diary
of
1/5th N. Lan. R.
for period
1st November to 30th November 1916

Army Form C. 2118.

1/5th. Loyal North Lancs. Regt.

# WAR DIARY
## or
## INTELLIGENCE SUMMARY.
(Erase heading not required.)

Instructions regarding War Diaries and Intelligence Summaries are contained in F. S. Regs., Part II. and the Staff Manual respectively. Title pages will be prepared in manuscript.

| Place | Date | Hour | Summary of Events and Information | Remarks and references to Appendices |
|---|---|---|---|---|
| TRENCHES YPRES. C.28.a.70.10to C.29.b.25.25. Reference Map. Secret M.1.19 | 1st.November, 1916 | | (38th Div. on our Left, 5th King's Own on our Right.) 2/Lieut. J.S.Carr proceeded to ETAPLES for tour of duty as Instructor. | |
| | 4th November, 1916. | | "A" and "B" Companies relieved "C" and "D" Companies respectively in front line trench system. | |
| | 6th Nov. 1916. | | Casualty:- 2129 Private Bradley, J. "B" Company, wounded. | |
| | 8th " " | | Battalion relieved by 1/10th (Scottish) Bn. King's Liverpool Regt Moved to CANAL BANK where in consequence of the bad weather many of the dugouts were not habitable, and much earth had fallen. Casualty:- 1617 Private Hutchinson,S. "C" Coy. Wounded at duty. | |
| | 9th " " | | 2/Lieut.E.Harling proceeded to HESDEN to join R.F.C. | |
| | 15th " " | | CASUALTY:- 8658 Private Taylor,J. "B" Coy. Wounded. | |
| | 16th " " | | Provided large party of 1 Officer and 150 Other ranks wiring front of WIELTJE POST, from 6 p.m. to 2 a.m. | |
| | 17th " " | | Battalion relieved by 1/8th (Irish) Bn.King's LiverpoolRgt. and moved by train from YPRES to "G" CAMP BRANDHOEK. Relief completed 7-20 p.m. Brigadier expressed his satisfaction and thanks for the wiring done on night of 16th | |
| | 18th " " | | Moved to "E" Camp, after evacuation of 9th King's Liverpool Regt. 1/10th Liverpool Scottish took over "G" Camp. | |
| | 19th " " | | Battalion commenced vigorous training. | |

Army Form C. 2118.

1/5th. Loyal North Lancs. Regt.

# WAR DIARY
# or
# INTELLIGENCE SUMMARY.
(Erase heading not required.)

Instructions regarding War Diaries and Intelligence Summaries are contained in F. S. Regs., Part II. and the Staff Manual respectively. Title pages will be prepared in manuscript.

| Place | Date | Hour | Summary of Events and Information | Remarks and references to Appendices |
|---|---|---|---|---|
| TRENCHES, YPRES. | 21st Nov. 1916. | | Ordinary Leave commenced. Battalion allotment - 3 vacancies daily. Period of leave to be 10 days from Port to Port. | |
| | 23rd. | " | Casualty - 1555 Private Clark, G. "C" Coy. G.S.W.thigh. Brig.Gen. inspected Battalion in Drill Order at 10 a.m. | |
| | 24th | " | Trial alarm during afternoon. Battalion and 1st. Line Transport turned out for the operation, and were inspected by the Divisional Commander. Casualty:- 1556 Private Clark, W. "B" Coy. Wounded. | |
| | 25th | " | Inspection of Brigades by Corps Commander cancelled on account of inclement weather. | |
| | 26th | " | Battalion left "B" Camp and entrained at BRANDHOEK at 5 p.m. detraining at YPRES 5-35 p.m. Relieved 1/8th (Irish) Bn. King's Lpl.Rgt. on CANAL BANK. Relief completed 7 p.m. | |
| | 27th | " | Battalion relieved 2/5th Lancs. Fusrs. in left subsector of left Brigade sector as follows:- <br>"C" Coy. in Front line, Right subsector. <br>"D" " " " " Left subsector. <br>"B" " " Support line. "A" Coy. in ST.JEAN. <br>Relief completed 8 p.m. <br>Casualty:- 826 Private Jones, G. "G" Coy.G.S.W.Right Hand. | |
| | 29th | " | Party of Liverpool Scottish successfully raided KAISER BILL and trenches in its vicinity (Trench Map ST.JULIEN 1/10,000 C.29.) about 5 p.m. after powerful Artillery preparation. Much information was obtained, prisoners were taken, many casualties caused, and much damage done to enemy trenches. Scottish casualties slight. During bombardment enemy retaliated on Normouth street. Casualties:- 1962 D.D.&LWe.Alb.Ss. F-m.C.Gr.8. Wounded, Shrapnell | |

Army Form C. 2118

1/5th. Loyal North Lancs. Regt.

# WAR DIARY
## or
## INTELLIGENCE SUMMARY
*(Erase heading not required.)*

Instructions regarding War Diaries and Intelligence Summaries are contained in F. S. Regs., Part II. and the Staff Manual respectively. Title Pages will be prepared in manuscript.

| Place | Date | Hour | Summary of Events and Information | Remarks and references to Appendices |
|---|---|---|---|---|
| TRENCHES, YPRES. | 30th Nov. 1916. | | "A" and "B" Companies relieved "C" and "D" Companies in front line in left and right subsectors respectively. Casualty:- 1657 Private Pratt, J. "D" Company. Wounded, Shrapnel. | |

J. Jones Major
O.C. 1/5th N. Lanc. R.

Vol 17

War Diary
of
1/5th N. Lan. R.
for period
December 1st – 31st 1916.

CONFIDENTIAL

# WAR DIARY
## or
## INTELLIGENCE SUMMARY
*(Erase heading not required.)*

Army Form C. 2118

1/5 L.N. LANCS. R.

Instructions regarding War Diaries and Intelligence Summaries are contained in F.S. Regs., Part II. and the Staff Manual respectively. Title Pages will be prepared in manuscript.

| Place | Date | Hour | Summary of Events and Information | Remarks and references to Appendices |
|---|---|---|---|---|
| TRENCHES. ST. JEAN. C.28.c.70.10.<br>C.29.b.25.25.<br>Secret Map W.1.19. | 1st December 1916. | | 38th Division on our LEFT.<br>1/5th South Lancs. Regt. on our RIGHT. | |
| | 2nd December 1916. | | Battalion relieved by 1/10th Liverpool Scottish, and went into dugouts on YSER CANAL. "Gas" Exercise carried out. | |
| | 3rd. December 1916 | | Casualty, No. 2054 Pte.Laycock,J. "D" Coy. Wounded Shrapnel Right arm. | |
| | 4th December 1916. | | No. 2545 L/Cpl.Sheppard,F. interviewed by Divisional Cmdr. re Commission. Not recommended on account of insufficient duty experience. | |
| | 5th December 1916. | | Brig.Gen.H.Green Wilkinson held conference of officers at Battalion Headquarters at 3 p.m. | |
| | 7th December 1916. | | Battalion relieved 1/10th (Scottish) Bn. K.L.R. in Front Line System.<br>"C" and "D" Companies in Front line, left and right subsectors respectively.<br>"A" Company in LIVERPOOL TRENCH. "B" Company in ST. JEAN.<br>Casualty, 3008 Pte.Wales,T. "C" Coy. Wounded. | |
| | 8th December 1916. | | Casualty, 3695 Pte.Edge,R. "A" Coy. Wounded. | |
| | 9th December 1916. | | "A" & "B" Coys. relieved "C" & "D" Coys.respectively in Front line trenches.<br>Casualty, 4762 Pte.Lacky,J. "B" Coy. Wounded. | |
| | 10th December 1916. | | Enemy shelled BILGE TRENCH heavily during morning and again in evening. Trench badly knocked about, several casualties suffered by "A" Coy. as a result.<br>Divisional Shoot arranged for artillery and machine guns at intervals until 9-35 p.m. | |

Army Form C. 2118

1/5th L.N.LANCS. R.

# WAR DIARY
# INTELLIGENCE SUMMARY
*(Erase heading not required.)*

Instructions regarding War Diaries and Intelligence Summaries are contained in F. S. Regs., Part II. and the Staff Manual respectively. Title Pages will be prepared in manuscript.

| Place | Date | Hour | Summary of Events and Information | Remarks and references to Appendices |
|---|---|---|---|---|
| | 10th December 1916. (continued). | | The fire was directed on enemy communication trenches and approaches to front line. Germans retaliating on our front line.<br>Casualties, 2539 L/Cpl.Oakes, A. "A" Coy. Killed in action<br>2426 M/Cpl.Till, I. "A" " " "<br>9 Other ranks wounded,<br>4 At duty, 1 died of wounds. | |
| | 11th December 1916. | | "A" Coy. again heavily shelled in ELLGE TRENCH. Casualties, 2/Lieut.C.B.Wray, "/Lieut.G.E.Ridding, - at duty. 7 Other ranks wounded. | |
| | 12th December 1916. | | Battalion relieved in front line system by 1/10th (Scottish) Bn. K.L.R., and moved to CANAL BANK. | |
| | 15th December 1916. | | Casualty, 6780 Pte.Gardner,C. "C" Coy. (Since died of wounds). 2737 " Graham,G. "A" Coy. Wounded. | |
| | 17th December 1916. | | Battalion relieved by 2/5th Lancashire Fusiliers, and proceeded to ASYLUM, YPRES, where we entrained. Detraining at VLAMERTINGHE 8 p.m. Marched to "B" Camp. | |
| | 18th December 1916. | | 2/Lieut.C.B.Coldham proceeded to VIII Corps Musketry Camp, to undertake duties of Camp Adjutant & Quartermaster. | |
| | 19th December 1916. | | Battalion prepared for inspection by G.O.C.-in-Chief, but inspection cancelled. | |
| | 20th December 1916. | | 2/Lts.W.M.Barrett, F.Dey, and J.M.Smart proceeded to join 16th Bn. Manchester Regiment. | |

1/5th LN LNCS R.

Army Form C. 2118

# WAR DIARY
## or
## INTELLIGENCE SUMMARY

*(Erase heading not required.)*

Instructions regarding War Diaries and Intelligence Summaries are contained in F. S. Regs., Part II. and the Staff Manual respectively. Title Pages will be prepared in manuscript.

| Place | Date | Hour | Summary of Events and Information | Remarks and references to Appendices |
|---|---|---|---|---|
| | 21st December 1916. | | 61 Other ranks proceeded to VIII Corps Musketry Camp by rail, to fire Parts III and IV of Musketry Course. Commander-in-Chief, General Sir Douglas Haig visited 166 Brigade area and camps, but did not inspect battalions as was intended, on account of inclement weather. | |
| | 24th December 1916. | | Divisional Commander interviewed the following N.C.O's. applicants for Commissions:- Nos. 3060 Cpl.Pickering,G., 3957 L/C.Carroll,L., 2518 L/C.Hamer,S., 2327 Sgt.Rousell,W.S. 2356 L/Sgt.Rawcliffe,J., 2544 L/Sgt.Pickering,F. | |
| | 25th December 1916. | | CHRISTMAS DAY - General Holiday. All N.C.O's. and men entertained to special Christmas dinner. | |
| | 28th December 1916. | | Divisional Commander inspected Lewis Guns during morning. The w/m. N.C.O's. proceeded to England as candidates for Commissions:- Nos.3060 Cpl. Pickering,G., 3957 L/C.Carroll,L. 2518 L/C.Hamer,S., 2327 Sgt.Rousell,W.S., 2356 L/Sgt. Rawcliffe,J., 2544 L/Sgt.Pickering,F. Battalion entrained at BRANDHOEK at 4-30 p.m. Detrained YPRES 5-0 p.m. Relieved D/10th (Scottish) K.L.R. on YSER CANAL BANK. Relief completed 7-0 p.m. | |
| | 31st.December 1916. | | Cpl.R.E.Pye proceeded to Divisional Reinforcement Camp as Acting Orderly Room Sergeant. L/Sgt.Jackson, to 166 Infantry Brigade as Acting Quartermaster Sergeant. | |

J.H.
Lt. Col.
Cmdg. 1/5th Loyal North Lancs. Regt.

Vol 18

War Diary
of the
1/5 N. Lan. R.
for the period
1/1/17 to 31/1/17.

Army Form C. 2118

# WAR DIARY
## or
## INTELLIGENCE SUMMARY
*(Erase heading not required.)*

Instructions regarding War Diaries and Intelligence Summaries are contained in F. S. Regs., Part II. and the Staff Manual respectively. Title Pages will be prepared in manuscript.

1/5th ROYAL NORTH LANCASHIRE BATTN.

| Place | Date | Hour | Summary of Events and Information | Remarks and references to Appendices |
|---|---|---|---|---|
| YPRES CANAL BANK. YPRES. | 1st January 1917. | | 12 N.C.O's. and men (Registered Tradesmen) interviewed by Committee of Interviewers at POPERINGHE. 2/Lieuts. D.B. Hamilton and R.D.Knowles joined Battalion for duty from England. Casualty - 3023 Pte. Yates,R. P.S./I. Stomach. | |
| | 2nd January 1917. | | Relieved 1/10th (Scottish) Bn. King's Liverpool Regt. in trenches as per margin. | |
| C.28.c.70.10. C.29.b.25.25 Secret map 7.1.19. | | | to 55th Division on Left, 5th(King's Own)R.L.Regt. | |
| | 3rd January 1917. | | 56 O.R. returned from VIIIth Corps Musketry Camp, having fired Course. | |
| | 5th January 1917. 7th January 1917. | | Casualty - Wounded - 2690 Pte. Riley, both thighs. Battalion relieved in trenches by 1/10th (Scottish) K.L.R. Rest. and moved to YSER CANAL BANK. | |
| | 8th January 1917. | | All available men, excluding Raiding Party employed on fatigues. | |
| | 9th January 1917. | | Raiding Party under Lieut. Wakant practised final rehearsal of Raid in presence of Divisional Commander on ground near PRISON, YPRES. The Div.Cmdr. expressed his approval of the display. Casualty - 2/Lieut. E.F. Wood, wounded, /.S.W. back. | |
| | 10th January 1917. | | Party of 5 officers (Lieut. Wakant, 2/Lieut. Frankland, & 2/Lt. Whitaker) and 140 O.R. attempted Raid on German trenches from C.29.a.38.80. to C.23.c.32.03., French Map 1/10,000 ST. JULIEN | |

Army Form C. 2118

# WAR DIARY
## or
## INTELLIGENCE SUMMARY
*(Erase heading not required.)*

| Place | Date | Hour | Summary of Events and Information | Remarks and references to Appendices |
|---|---|---|---|---|
| | 10th January 1917 | | **1/5th LOYAL NORTH LANCASHIRE REGIMENT** | |

(continued).

Party divided into two - left and right.
Lieut. Melsent in command of left party.
2/Lieut. Frankland " " right "
2/Lieut. Whitaker in Reserve.
Left Party assembled in Scottish trench, and right party in PROMIS TRENCH at 5 p.m.
Artillery bombardment commenced at 3-10 p.m.
Parties left assembly trenches at 4-40 p.m., and proceeded in file to front line, crossing front line at 5 p.m. exactly, and taking up a position in FIRST DITCH in "NO MAN'S LAND"; *then going on to SECOND DITCH.*
Emerged from SECOND DITCH at 5-15 p.m. - ZERO hour - and made for German trenches as per programme. Right party on reaching enemy wire found it uncut, and encountered heavy machine gun fire from KAISER RILL on their right front.
It was impossible for this party to enter enemy trenches, and it sustained many casualties, 2/Lieut. Whitaker finally giving the order for the party to withdraw - 2/Lieut. Frankland had been killed earlier in the engagement -.
The left party was successful in effecting an entry into the German trenches at G.29.a.27.98., meeting with very little opposition until inside the trench where stubborn resistance was encountered. Many of the enemy were killed, and two dugouts and an O.P. bombed. A bugle call, "G", was the signal for our parties to withdraw. The enemy appeared to be in strength, and well prepared for the raid. They fought bravely, and although our Artillery and T.M.bombardment was heavy, VERY lights and rocket signals were sent up regularly throughout the operations. The German artillery barrage was particularly heavy - there was a marked increase in their retaliatory fire as compared with previous minor operations in this sector.
Our casualties were - Officers - Killed 2/Lieut. J.C.Frankland
  wounded 2/Lieut.C.W.Whitaker
  2/Lieut. Alan Jones.
Other ranks - killed 7 - Wounded 48 (3 at duty).
  missing 2.

Army Form C. 2118

# WAR DIARY
## or
## INTELLIGENCE SUMMARY
*(Erase heading not required.)*

Instructions regarding War Diaries and Intelligence Summaries are contained in F. S. Regs., Part II. and the Staff Manual respectively. Title Pages will be prepared in manuscript.

1/5th LOYAL NORTH LANCASHIRE REGIMENT.

| Place | Date | Hour | Summary of Events and Information | Remarks and references to Appendices |
|---|---|---|---|---|
| | 12th January 1917. | | Billeting party consisting of Q.M. and 4 other Ranks proceeded to VOLKERINGHOVE to arrange for billets for Battalion. 4 Officers from 1/1st Cambridgeshire Regt. (relieving unit) attached until relief. | |
| | 13th January 1917. | | Battalion relieved by 1/1st Cambridgeshire Regt., 59th Division. Relief complete 7 p.m. Battalion entrained at YPRES, and on detrainment at BRANDHOEK marched to "O" Camp for night. Captain Harris, Lieut. Sparkes and 2/Lieut. Curtis joined Battalion for duty from England. Casualty - 2257 Cpl. Russell, G. Wounded, shell, finger, slight at duty. | |
| | 14th January 1917. | | Battalion paraded in Column of Route outside "O" Camp at 10-50 a.m. and marched to Ouderezeerzeel Station, POPERINGHE. Entrained at 1-50 p.m., travelled by rail to Brigade Training Area. Detrained at POLLINKHOVE 4-35 p.m. and marched to VOLKERINGHOVE, where Battalion was billeted. The 166 Brigade was distributed as under:-<br>POPERINGHE, Brigade H.Q., 1/5th King's Own (R.L.) Regt. and 1/10th (Scottish) Bn. King's Lpl. Regt.<br>LARCH HILL, 1/5th South Lancs. Regt.<br>VOLKERINGKOVE, 1/5th Loyal North Lancs. Regt. | |
| | 15th January 1917. | | Men occupied cleaning themselves generally. | |
| | 16th January 1917. | | Commenced training on Brigade training ground. All details made up to establishment. | |
| | 19th January 1917. | | 2/Lieut. J.J.Crabtree joined Battalion for duty from 1/4th L.N.L.R. | |

Army Form C. 2118

# WAR DIARY
# -of-
# INTELLIGENCE SUMMARY

(Erase heading not required.)

Instructions regarding War Diaries and Intelligence Summaries are contained in F.S. Regs., Part II. and the Staff Manual respectively. Title Pages will be prepared in manuscript.

1/5th LOYAL NORTH LANCASHIRE REGIMENT.

| Place | Date | Hour | Summary of Events and Information | Remarks and references to Appendices |
|---|---|---|---|---|
| | 20th January 1917. | | Reinforcement of 7 O.R. rejoined from BASE. | |
| | 22nd January 1917. | | Captain A.I. Morris returned to his own unit, 1/4th L.N.Lan.R. | |
| | 23rd January 1917. | | Draft 6 N.C.O's. (King's Rpl.Regt.) joined Battalion from Base. Armourer Sergeant joined Battalion. | |
| | 24th January 1917. | | The u/m N.C.O's. proceeded to England for Commissions:- <br> 752 C.Q.M.S. Garline, M. <br> 2458 Sgt. Berrett, J.G. <br> 2378 L/Sgt. Roberts, N. | |
| | 28th January 1917. | | 2/Lieut. A.D. Caborner left Battalion. | |
| | 29th January 1917. | | 1749 Sgt. McLarty interviewed by Brigade and Divisional Commanders re Commission. | |
| | 30th January 1917. | | relief <br> Intended of 164 Brigade by 166th Brigade in area near WIALENTIGNY on this day, cancelled until further orders. Final tie in Rifle Competition (Battalion) between "A" and "D" Companies, decided - "D" Company victors. | |
| | 31st January 1917. | | Army Commander visited Training Area. <br> "D" Company won the honour of representing 166 Brigade in Divisional Rifle Competition by defeating 1/5th South Lan.R. and 1/10th (Scottish) K.L.R. | |

Sgd. [signature] Capt. for Capt.
Cmdg. 1/5th Loyal North Lancs. Regt.

5 LNL January 1917

Preliminary Report on Raid carried out by
the 1/5th L.N.Lan.Regt., 166th Infantry
Brigade on the afternoon of the 10th
January 1917.
********************

The bombardment by the Heavy Artillery and the Divisional Artillery started according to programme. At first retaliation by the enemy was slight. His Artillery was assisted by two aeroplanes which flew rather lower than usual over our lines. Towards 5 p.m. the enemy Artillery became more active, our front line South of WIELTJE receiving most attention.

The Raiding parties 'A' and 'B' advanced respectively from PROWSE and LONE FARMS and reached the rendezvous, (the ditch running South-East from ARGYLE FARM), with few casualties.

The Right Party 'A' in its advance from the rendezvous lost its Bangalore Torpedo party by shell fire, and the wire being found insufficiently cut, no entry was possible. The Officer in Command, who was wounded, decided to withdraw his party. His scouts had found the German parapet manned and were bombed by the enemy, thus preventing the wire being cut by hand.

The Left party 'B' found the wire well cut and entered the German trenches; they were immediately met by opposition. They were bombed and owing to the darkness were unable to ascertain the direction from which the bombs were coming. About eight Germans were encountered and these were killed. They showed no inclination to surrender.

The party succeeded in destroying two concrete dugouts. Owing to increased opposition and the difficulty of exercising control in the darkness the progress was very slow, and when the signal for retirement was given it had only succeeded in penetrating about 50 yards. This party brought back identifications of the 162nd Infantry Regt. No prisoners were taken.

There was a marked increase of hostile Artillery as compared with other raids carried out by this Division on this front, which greatly handicapped the operations.

The bombardment of the enemy's trenches immediately North of the YPRES-ROULERS Railway at first, no doubt, deceived the enemy as to the intention of the operations as at first he replied with a fairly heavy barrage, which gradually slackened off.

After Zero an Officers' patrol sent to ascertain the damage done to the enemy's trenches reported a lane cut through the enemy's wire at I6c 15.55 and the front trenches in the locality appeared to be much damaged, but the patrol was prevented from making a close reconnaissance owing to their presence being discovered and subsequently being fired on by Machine Guns.

The casualties were as follows :-

Officers.

Killed.   1.
Wounded   1.

Other Ranks.

Killed.   7.
Wounded.  49.
Missing
(believed killed) 4.

55th Division No. ~~1143/21~~ (G).

GENERAL STAFF
HEADQUARTERS
8th CORPS.

No. 55468

Date.

VIII Corps.
----------

With reference to the preliminary report on raid last night by 1/5th Loyal North Lancashire Regiment forwarded under 55th Division No. 1143/19 (G) of 10/1/17. I submit at once the following deductions in case any similar enterprises are in contemplation in the near future. If any further lessons come to light they will be brought to your notice.

1. We must now expect a heavier barrage to be developed by the enemy than we have been used to lately. Accurate location of the enemy's batteries and careful counter-battery work will be a necessity in future raids. The enemy has become accustomed to being raided on this front, and knows what to expect when our artillery fire becomes intense. His artillery are likely to be registered on ground in front of the trenches bombarded and to be ready for immediate action.

2. Our artillery was somewhat inconvenienced by hostile aeroplanes, which were enabled to observe and spot our batteries without difficulty owing to the absence of our aircraft. His own planes seem to have increased in number lately. It therefore seems desirable in such operations in future to send up planes to keep his at a distance.

H. S. Jeudwine
Major General.

55th Div. H.Q.
11th January 1917.
Commanding 55th Division.

1.  Were the aeroplanes sufficiently engaged by the A.A. Guns?

2.  Why were no arrangements made for understudies to the Torpedo party?  Were spare torpedoes carried?

3.  Was failure to cut the wire on the Right due to the casualties in the T.M. Batteries?  What were these casualties?  Did the 18 pdrs. do their share of wire cutting?

4.  The scouts of the Right party found the German parapet manned.  It appears therefore that the raiding party were not sufficiently close up to the barrage.  In both cases the enemy were evidently not much shaken by our Artillery fire.

5.  At what stage were the heaviest casualties incurred - before the raid, during the stay in the enemy's trenches or during withdrawal?

55th Division No. 1/43/24(G).

VIII Corps.
----------

By direction of the Corps Commander I submit the following notes, in addition to those already forwarded, on points on which experience has been gained in recent raids made by this Division..

1. <u>Wire cutting</u>. The surest and most effective way of cutting wire is with 18-prs or Medium Trench Mortars.

Of these 18-prs are the most generally applicable. Provided the wire can be observed it can always be cut by them.

Medium Trench Mortars with Newton fuze are equally good if suitable positions can be found for them. But owing to their limited range and the fact that the ground immediately behind our front line is generally under observation by the enemy this is often difficult. An additional difficulty is the nature of the soil on our front, which is so soft as to necessitate rather elaborate preparation of beds. If trench mortars are located by the enemy, which is easy for him if they fire much in the daylight, owing to their necessary proximity to the front line, they are very likely to be knocked out before they can achieve their object. When they are used for wire cutting it is therefore desirable that they shall not fire longer by daylight than is necessary for them to range on their objective. It has been found that they can generally do this by commencing fire from ten to twenty minutes before sundown.

In the case of both 18-prs and Medium Trench Mortars a clear view of the enemy's wire is essential.

2. <u>Aeroplanes</u>. I have already brought to notice the

advisability

advisability of detailing planes to keep the enemy's planes at a distance during our bombardment. This has become more important owing to the increase of hostile planes on our front. It may also be desirable specially to warn our anti-aircraft guns to be on the look out, and perhaps to detail some to forward positions.

### Box barrage.

3. It would appear that in some cases where a box barrage has been used the sides of the box have not had sufficiently intense fire to render them impassable, and consequently flank attacks by the enemy have been possible on the raiding party after it has penetrated. This has increased their difficulties and caused time to be occupied in resisting a flank attack which should have been devoted to exploring the region bombarded.

4. Degree of bombardment. Unless it is intended to make a regular attack, over the ground, to the support line, it is probably best not to obliterate too completely the communication trenches leading to it. If they are thoroughly blown in it is difficult for parties which have to work up them to recognize them, and moreover these parties have to work in the open, and form an easy target to enemy rifles and machine guns from surrounding trenches. It is probably best to obliterate thoroughly the trenches round the locality to be raided, so that cover is denied to the enemy, while dealing only sufficiently severely with those inside the area to shake the nerves of any enemy who may be in them.

5. Programme. We have raided the enemy so often that in gaining experience ourselves we have also educated him. If he gets a hint of our intention he is likely to be prepared. It is therefore inadvisable to cut wire or bombard long before a raid, leaving an interval of tranquillity in which he can prepare and organise his

/defence

Bombardment and wire cutting once begun should continue until the assault is launched.

6. <u>Duplication of appliances etc.</u>, Anything or any party may be and often is knocked out by shell fire before reaching the place where it is to be used. <u>Everything</u> should therefore as far as possible be duplicated, and so placed that the duplicates are not likely both to be damaged. In the last raid owing to difficulties of observation the guns and trench mortars failed to cut the enemy's wire completely at one point of entry. Bangalore torpedos had been prepared in duplicate, each with duplicate means of firing. But the two parties carrying the torpedos moved together, and both were knocked out by a single shell before they could get to the enemy's wire. The party was unable to effect an entry.

55th Division H.Q.,
11th January 1917.

Major General
Commanding 55th Division.

CONFIDENTIAL

Vol 19

War Diary
of
1/5th N.Lan.R
for the period
1st to 28th February 1917

Army Form C. 2118.

1/5th Bn. Loyal North Lancs. Regt.

# WAR DIARY
*or*
## INTELLIGENCE SUMMARY.

*(Erase heading not required.)*

Instructions regarding War Diaries and Intelligence Summaries are contained in F.S. Regs., Part II. and the Staff Manual respectively. Title pages will be prepared in manuscript.

| Place | Date | Hour | Summary of Events and Information | Remarks and references to Appendices |
|---|---|---|---|---|
| VOLKERINCKHOVE. | 1st February 1917. | | | |
| | 2nd February 1917. | | Billeting party under 2nd Lt. P. O. Davies proceeded to "D" Camp, VLAMERTINGHE, to take over from 1/4th Kings Own. Battalion proceeded on Route march in Easterly direction from 3 p.m. to 4.30 p.m. and then returned for stragetic purposes. Billeting party of 2/5th Lancs. Fusuliers arrived to take over billets. | |
| "D" CAMP, BRANDHOEK. | 3rd February 1917. | | Battalion paraded outside "A" Coy. Headquarters at 7.40 a.m. and marched to BOLLEZEELE entraining 9.10 a.m. Detrained POPERINGHE 1.15 p.m. and marched to "D" Camp on ELVERDINGHE ROAD. Attached to 164th Infantry Brigade in reserve to 38th Division. | |
| | 4th February 1917. | | 166th Brigade took over "D" Camp, relieving 164th Brigade. | |
| | 6th February 1917. | | Test alarm "READY" given at 2 p.m. Battalion ready to move 2.40 p.m. | |
| | 7th February 1917. | | Test alarm given at 2 p.m. for Lewis Gun limbers and chargers. Horses hitched in limbers ready to move 2.34 pm. | |
| | 9th February 1917. | | "B" and "D" Companies relieved "C" and "B" Companies 5th Kings Own (R.L.R.) on CANAL BANK, YPRES. Relief completed 9.0 p.m. | |
| | 10th February 1917. | | Lewis gun limbers inspected by Brigadier General at 3 p.m. | |
| | 11th February 1917. | | Brigadier General presented Medal ribbons to; Lt. R.K. Makant, Bar to M.C., Sgt. Robinson, M.M., L/Sgt.Howarth G. M.M., Pte. J. Lane, M.M., R. S. M. A. Watts, M.C. | |
| | 12th February 1917. | | 2nd Lt. J. A. Jones returned to duty from Base. | |

Army Form C. 2118.

# WAR DIARY
## or
## INTELLIGENCE SUMMARY.

*(Erase heading not required.)*

Instructions regarding War Diaries and Intelligence Summaries are contained in F. S. Regs., Part II. and the Staff Manual respectively. Title pages will be prepared in manuscript.

| Place | Date | Hour | Summary of Events and Information | Remarks and references to Appendices |
|---|---|---|---|---|
| | 14th February 1917. | | Capt. A.A.Turner(R.A.M.C.) reported to 1/3 West Lancs. F. Ambulance for duty and was replaced by Lt. J. A. McIlroy. | |
| | 15th February 1917. | | 1708 Sgt. McLarty proceeded to England for Commission. | |
| | 16th February 1917. | | Draft of 17 other ranks joined from Reinforcement Camp. (originally in 3rd Bn. West Kents Regt.) | |
| YPRES, CANAL BANK. | 17th February 1917. | | Relieved 1/1st Herts. Regt. on CANAL BANK, YPRES. Moved from "D" Camp at 5.45 p.m., entrained BRANDHOEK 7.0p.m. Relief complete 9.0p.m. 2nd Lt. Wood returned to duty from Base. | |
| | 20th February 1917. | | 7769 Pte. Shaw T. "D" Company (attached 177 Tunnelling Coy) wounded, back, shell. | |
| 21st February TRENCHES. C28.a.70.10. C29.b.25.25. Secret Map W.L.19. | 21st February 1917. | | Relieved 1/10th Liverpool Scottish Regt., in WIELTJE SECTOR "C" Company, Front Line. "A" Company, BILGE TRENCH. "G" Company, LIVERPOOL TRENCH. "D" Company, ST JEAN. Relief completed 8.30 p.m. Capt. Chronnell proceeded to VIII Corps S.O.T.C. 1/5th South Lancs. on the right, 39th Division on the left. | |
| | 22nd February 1917. | | 5 men proceeded to Transport Depot, BOULOGNE for Duty. 909 Sgt. Lawler proceeded to 2nd Army Musketry School as Sergt. Major. | |
| | 23rd February 1917. | | 2nd Lieut. C.B.Coagham rejoined unit. | |
| | 24th February 1917. | | Firing team of "B" Coy. won the Cup offered by Sir Evelyn Wood, to 55th Division, beating 1/4th L.North Lancs. R. (representatives 164 Brigade) in Semi-final by 12 points | |

Army Form C. 2118.

# WAR DIARY
## or
## INTELLIGENCE SUMMARY

*(Erase heading not required.)*

Instructions regarding War Diaries and Intelligence Summaries are contained in F.S. Regs., Part II. and the Staff Manual respectively. Title pages will be prepared in manuscript.

| Place | Date | Hour | Summary of Events and Information | Remarks and references to Appendices |
|---|---|---|---|---|
| | 24th February 1917. | | Continued. and 5th Kings (Liverpool) Regt., (representatives 165 Brigade) in the final by 9 points to 8. Team consisted of:- <br>1890 Cpl. Hoole W.    2102 L/C. Prendergrast J. <br>1864 Pte. Cartwright.    2832 Pte. Roberts T. <br>2010 " Boardman J.    7456 " Cox T. <br>1820 " Harvey H.    3519 " Hetherington W. <br>2041 " Bradshaw F.    3417 " Thompson G. <br>2232 " Rothwell W.    1271 " Parkinson H. | |
| | 25th February 1917. | | 8677 Pte. Nuttall H. "B" Coy., (attached 177 Tunnelling Coy) wounded. | |
| "B" CAMP, BRANDHOEK. | 26th February 1917. | | Battalion Relieved by 2/5th Lancs. Fusuliers in ST JEAN and proceeded to YPRES (H.12.C) where we entrained at 11.0p.m Detrained BRANDHOEK and proceeded to usual quarters at "B" Camp. <br>Casualty:- 3107 Pte. Bullough F. "A" Company - Shell wound head. | |
| | 27th February 1917. | | 2nd Lt. Udall, 2nd Lt. J.A.Jones, 2nd Lt. C.B.Wray, 1890 Cpl. Hoole W., 1361 Cpl. Gregson E., proceeded on Course of Instruction to 55th Division School. Commenced Training. | |
| | 28th February 1917. | | 1 other rank proceeded to Transport Depot, BOULOGNE for duty. 28 other ranks of 3/5th L. North Lancs. Regt. joined Battn. for duty. | |
| | 1st March 1917. | | | |

B. Long. Capt.

O.C. 1/5th Loyal N. Lancs. Regt.

Lieut-Col.
1/5th Loyal N. Lancs. Regt.

Vol 20

War Diary
of the
1/5th N. Lan. R.
for the period
1st to 31st March,
1917.

Army Form C. 2118

1/5th Loyal North Lancashire Regiment.

# WAR DIARY
# INTELLIGENCE SUMMARY

(Erase heading not required.)

Instructions regarding War Diaries and Intelligence Summaries are contained in F.S. Regs, Part II. and the Staff Manual respectively. Title Pages will be prepared in manuscript.

| Place | Date | Hour | Summary of Events and Information | Remarks and references to Appendices |
|---|---|---|---|---|
| "B" Camp, BRANDHOEK. | 1st March 1917. | | | |
| | 2nd March 1917. | | 28 Other ranks joined Battalion from Base (originally in 4th Battn. East Surrey Regt.) CASUALTY - No. 4232 Pte. Kelly,H., accidentally wounded by a bomb. | |
| | 4th March 1917. | | 21 Other ranks joined Battalion from Base for duty. "D" Company inspected by Brig. Gen. L.Green Wilkinson at 10-15 a.m. 2/Lieut. G.B.Coldham proceeded to Second Army Musketry School for duty as Adjutant and Quartermaster. | |
| | 6th March 1917. | | One Lewis Gun Limber, loaded, with team, proceeded to VIIIth Corps.S.O.T.S. for inspection by Corps Commander. | |
| CONVENT, YPRES. | 7th March 1917. | | Battalion entrained at BRANDHOEK at 10-0 p.m. Detrained at ASYLUM, YPRES at 10-20 p.m. and proceeded to billets in CONVENT, YPRES. | |
| | 11th March 1917. | | 2/Lieut. A.W.Jones injured by fall of bricks caused by British gun fire (wounded). | |
| | 12th March 1917. | | Brig. Gen. L.Green Wilkinson interviewed the following N.C.O's, applicants for Commissions:- L/Sgt.Wells,F., L/Cpl.Mowle,R.B., L/Cpl.Harrison,E. L/Cpl.Hamer,J.E. Relieved 1/10th (Scottish) Bn. King's Liverpool Regt. in POTIJZE SECTOR. "B" Coy. Right Front. "D" Coy. Left Front. "C" Coy. Right Support. "A" Coy. Left Support. ........ Brigade on Left. | |

Army Form C. 2118

# WAR DIARY
## INTELLIGENCE SUMMARY
*(Erase heading not required.)*

Instructions regarding War Diaries and Intelligence
Summaries are contained in F. S. Regs., Part II.
and the Staff Manual respectively. Title Pages
will be prepared in manuscript.

| Place | Date | Hour | Summary of Events and Information | Remarks and references to Appendices |
|---|---|---|---|---|
| | 13th/MARCH 1917. | | 2/Lieut. R. Rees returned to duty from 177 Tunnelling Coy. | |
| | 16th March 1917. | | Capt. A. Entwisle and 2/Lieut. R.A. Thornley reported for duty from ENGLAND. CASUALTY – No.240045 Pte. Preston, J.T., Killed in action. | |
| PRISON, YPRES. 17th March 1917. | | | Battalion relieved by 1/9th King's Liverpool Regt., and proceed to billets in PRISON, YPRES. Relief complete, 10–30 p.m. | |
| | 21st/March 1917. | | 2/Lieut. M.H.Butt and 2/Lieut. J. Rainbow (3rd.L.N.Lancs.R.) joined Battalion for duty from ENGLAND. 18 Other ranks joined Battalion from Base. | |
| | 22nd March 1917. | | Relief of 1/10th (Scottish) Bn. King's Liverpool Regt. postponed one day presumably owing to possible betrayal of information by prisoners whom enemy took during a raid on our lines in POTIJZE SECTOR. | |
| TRENCHES. C.28.a.70.10. C.29.B.25.25. Secret Map W.L.19. | 23rd March 1917. | | Relieved 1/10th (Scottish) Bn. King's Liverpool Regt. in WIELTJE SECTOR. "A" Coy. Right Front. "C" " WIELTJE DEFENCES. "B" " BILGE TRENCH. "D" " LIVERPOOL TRENCH, CONGREVE WALK and ST. JEAN DEFENCES. Relief Complete 10–15 p.m. 166 Brigade on Right. 5th South Lancs. Regt. on Left. | |
| | 24th March 1917. | | "Summer Time" commences. Clocks and watches put forward from 11–0 p.m. to 12–0 midnight. | |
| | 26th March 1917. | | CASUALTIES – No.243809 Pte. Ward, A.; No.2441533 Pte. Lyon, H.; No.240196 Pte. McGee, J.; No.242704 Pte. Butler, G. 4/15 I.E.F.& A.F.D.S.S./Forms/C.2118.) Wounded. | |

1875 Wt. W593/826 1,000,000

# WAR DIARY
## INTELLIGENCE SUMMARY

*(Erase heading not required.)*

1/5th Loyal North Lancashire Regiment.

Army Form C. 2118

| Place | Date | Hour | Summary of Events and Information | Remarks and references to Appendices |
|---|---|---|---|---|
| | 26th March 1917. (cont.) | | CASUALTY - No. 241538 Pte. Crompton, T., wounded. | |
| | 28th March 1917. | | Relieved by 2/5th Lancashire Fusiliers in WIELTJE SECTOR. Relief complete 11-30 p.m. Proceeded to ASYLUM, thence and entrained at 1-0 a.m. 29th march. Detrained BRANDHOEK at 1-30 a.m., 29th, and occupied usual billets in "B" CAMP. | |
| | 29th March 1917. | | "B" CAMP. | |

for Captain Cmdg. 1/5th Loyal N. Lancs. Regt.    Captain.

CONFIDENTIAL

Vol 21

War Diary
of
1/5th N. Lan. R.
for the period
April 1st to 30th, 1917

Army Form C. 2118

# 1/5th Loyal North Lancashire Regiment.
## WAR DIARY
## or
## INTELLIGENCE SUMMARY
*(Erase heading not required.)*

Instructions regarding War Diaries and Intelligence Summaries are contained in F.S. Regs., Part II. and the Staff Manual respectively. Title Pages will be prepared in manuscript.

| Place | Date | Hour | Summary of Events and Information | Remarks and references to Appendices |
|---|---|---|---|---|
| "B" CAMP BRANDHOEK. | April 1st. 1917. | | Training continued. | |
| | April 4th 1917. | | Orderly Room Sergeant, No.240152 Sgt. Rigby,A., arrived from Base to check Records. | |
| | April 7th 1917. | | America declare war on Germany. | |
| | April 7th 1917. | | Test Gas Alarm carried out by 166th Infantry Brigade at 10-30 a.m. | |
| April 7th 1917. CONVENT, YPRES. | | | Relieved 1/10th (Scottish) Bn. King's Liverpool Regt. at CONVENT, YPRES. Entrained BRANDHOEK at 9-45 p.m., detrained ASYLUM, YPRES at 10-15 p.m. and proceeded to usual billets at CONVENT. | |
| | April 8th 1917. | | Lieut. R.W.B.Sparkes attached to Right Group Artillery for three days. | |
| | April 9th 1917. | | Remainder of the Tower of YPRES CATHEDRAL collapsed at 11 a.m. Commencement of ARRAS Offensive by First and Third Armies. | |
| | April 11th 1917. | | Orderly Room Sergeant, No.240152 Sgt. Rigby,A.,returned to Base. Lieut. R.W.B.Sparkes rejoined unit from attachment to Right Group Artillery. | |
| April 12th 1917. POTIJZE. | | | Relieved 1/10th (Scottish) Bn. King's Liverpool Regt. in POTIJZE Sector. Distribution as under:- <br> "B" Coy. Right Front. <br> "D" " Left Front. <br> "C" " Right Support. <br> "A" " Left Support. <br> Enemy shelled ST. JAMES' TRENCH during relief causing 6 casualties. 1/5th South Lancs.R. on Right, 164th Infantry Bde. on Left. | |

Army Form C. 2118

1/5th Loyal North Lancashire Regiment.

# WAR DIARY or INTELLIGENCE SUMMARY

(Erase heading not required.)

Instructions regarding War Diaries and Intelligence Summaries are contained in F.S. Regs., Part II. and the Staff Manual respectively. Title Pages will be prepared in manuscript.

| Place | Date | Hour | Summary of Events and Information | Remarks and references to Appendices |
|---|---|---|---|---|
| | April 13th 1917. | | Casualty - 1 other rank wounded. | |
| | April 15th 1917. | | Major G.D. Morton, 1/10th (Scottish) Bn. King's Liverpool Regt. attached to this unit for duty - took over Command of the Battalion. Captain F.W. Fawssett, R.A.M.C. joined Battalion for duty as Medical Officer vice Lieut. J.A. McIlroy. Casualties - 4 other ranks wounded - 1 accidentally, 3 at duty. | |
| | April 17th 1917. | | Major G.D. Morton proceed to VIIIth Corps S.O.T.S. for Course of Instruction. | |
| PRISON, YPRES. | | | Relieved by 1/7th King's Liverpool Regt. and 1/5th King's Own (Royal Lancaster Regt.) in POTIJZE Sector as per following dispositions :- <br> Right Front and Support taken over by 1/7th K.L.R. <br> Left Front and Support " " 1/5th King's Own <br> Headquarters - part taken over by each relieving Regiment. <br> Relief complete 11-30 p.m. Battalion billeted in PRISON. | |
| | April 18th 1917. | | Casualty - 1 other rank wounded, at duty. | |
| | April 19th 1917. | | Lieut. E.H. Ward rejoined Battalion for duty from England. Casualty - 1 other rank wounded, at duty. | |
| WIELTJE Sector | April 22nd 1917. | | Enemy shelled PRISON between 10-30 a.m. and 11-0 a.m. causing 9 casualties. <br> Major Morton returned from Course at VIIIth Corps S.O.T.S. Relieved 1/10th (Scottish) K.L.R. in WIELTJE Sector. <br> Dispositions :- "A" Coy. - Right Front <br> "C" " - Wieltje Defences <br> "D" " - BILGE TRENCH. <br> "B" " - CONGREVE WALK & LIVERPOOL TRENCH. <br> 1/5th King's Own (R.L.R.). 39th Division on Left. | |

1875  Wt. W593/826  1,000,000  4/15  J.B.C. & A.  A.D.S.S./Forms/C.2118.

Army Form C. 2118

1/5th Loyal North Lancashire Regiment.
WAR DIARY
or
INTELLIGENCE SUMMARY
(Erase heading not required.)

Instructions regarding War Diaries and Intelligence Summaries are contained in F.S. Regs., Part II. and the Staff Manual respectively. Title Pages will be prepared in manuscript.

| Place | Date | Hour | Summary of Events and Information | Remarks and references to Appendices |
|---|---|---|---|---|
| | April 22nd 1917. (continued) | | Casualties - No. 243915 Pte.Mitchell,S.W., killed in action<br>" 241435 " Maden,J. " " "<br>" 201472 " Hunter,W. " " "<br>2/Lt. C.B.Wray, wounded, at duty.<br>6 other ranks wounded.(2 at duty). | |
| | April 23rd 1917. | | Casualties - 2 other ranks wounded. | |
| | April 24th 1917. | | Lieut.Col. T.O.Smith rejoined Battalion from leave, and took over Command.<br>Hurricane bombardment by our Artillery at 10-0 p.m. Enemy retaliated on our front line extending from POTIJZE on right along whole of 39th Divisional front on left. | |
| | April 25th 1917. | | Brig. Gen. F.G.Lewis took over Command of 166th Infantry Brigade vice Brig. Gen. L.Green Wilkinson to England. | |
| PRISON, YPRES. | April 27th 1917. | | Relieved by 1/10th (Scottish) K.L.R. in WIELTJE Sector. Relief complete 11-0 p.m. Battalion proceed to usual billets in PRISON. | |

J. Smith
Lieut-Col.
Cmdg. 1/5th Loyal North Lancs. Regt.

Vol 22

CONFIDENTIAL

War Diary

of

1/5th N. Lan. R.

for the period

May 1st to 31st. 1917

Army Form C. 2118

1/5 LOYAL N.LANCS.RGT.

# WAR DIARY
or
## INTELLIGENCE SUMMARY
*(Erase heading not required.)*

Instructions regarding War Diaries and Intelligence Summaries are contained in F.S. Regs., Part II. and the Staff Manual respectively. Title Pages will be prepared in manuscript.

| Place | Date | Hour | Summary of Events and Information | Remarks and references to Appendices |
|---|---|---|---|---|
| YPRES | 1.5.17<br>2.5.17 | | Battalion billetted in PRISON.<br>"    "    "    "    "<br>Casualties. 3 O.R. wounded one of whom died of wounds. | |
| | 3.5.17 | | Battalion relieved 1/10 Liverpool(Scottish) Regt in the WIELTJE Sector.<br>Dispositions:- "D" Company   Right Front.<br>                "B"   "   WIELTJE DEFENCES.<br>                "C"   "   BILGE TRENCH.<br>                "A"   "   CONGREVE WALK.<br>Relief complete 11.35p.m.<br>Casualties.   4 O.R. wounded including 1 returned to duty.<br>In Trenches. ST.JEAN WAS frequently shelled during this tour in trenches.<br>Casualties:- 4th inst. 2 O.R. wounded.<br>             5th  "   2  "   "<br>             6th  "   1  "   "   including 1 R.T.D.<br>                "   "   1  "   "           1  " | |
| | 4.5.17 to<br>7.5.17 | | | |
| | 8.5.17 | | Battalion relieved by 2/5 Lancashire Fusiliers in WIELTJE Sector. Relief complete 11.50 p.m. Battalion entrained at YPRES and detrained POPERINGHE AT 1 p.m. Marched to "M" Camp near PROVEN.<br>Casualties:- 3 O.R. wounded. | |
| | 9.5.17 to<br>17.5.17 | | Training at "M" Camp<br>240086 Pte Parkinson H "B" Coy. killed in action whilst employed with TOWN MAJOR YPRES. 13.5.17. | |
| | 18.5.17 | | Battalion, less "B" Coy. remaining in PROVEN in billets for working purposes, marched from "M" camp to "B" Camp BRANDHOEK. arriving 5 p.m. | |
| | 19.5.17 to<br>25.5.17<br>25.5.17 | | Battalion in "B" Camp. 75% employed daily on Working parties. Remainder continued training.<br>Battalion entrained BRANDHOEK, detrained YPRES, and relieved portions of the 1/10 L'Pool Scottish Regt., 1/5 S.Lancs R. & 1/5 K.O.R.L. ,in support becoming the "SUPPORT WORKING BATTALION". | |

Army Form C. 2118

**1/5 LOYAL N.LANCS. RGT.**

**WAR DIARY**
or
**INTELLIGENCE SUMMARY**

(Erase heading not required.)

| Place | Date | Hour | Summary of Events and Information | Remarks and references to Appendices |
|---|---|---|---|---|
| | 25.5.17 | | Dispositions. | |
| | | | "B" COMPANY   ECOLE | |
| | | | "C"      "         " | |
| | | | "A"      "      ST.JAMES TR.     1 platoon. | |
| | | | "D"      "      Potijze.         1    " | |
| | | |                 HALF MOON TR.    1    " | |
| | | |                 HEDGE TRENCH     1    " | |
| | | | H.Q.            SOUTH LANE       2    " | |
| | | | 4 Lewis Guns and Teams attached to 1/5 S.Lancs.R. in front line. Relief complete 3.15 a.m. 26th inst. | |
| | 26.5.17 to 28.5.17 | | Battalion engaged on working parties day and night. Average strength of parties 300 to 350. | |
| | 29.5.17 | | Mine blown by R.E. in front of RAILWAY WOOD Sector at 10.30 p.m. Enemy took it very quietly. | |
| | 30.5.17 | | Still on working parties. Casualties:- 2 O.R. wounded. | |
| | 31.5.17 | | SOUTH LANE slightly shelled during afternoon. Casualties:- 2 O.R. wounded including 1 R.T.D. | |

[signature]
Lieut.-Col.,
Cmdg. 1/5 Loyal North Lancashire Regiment.

CONFIDENTIAL

War Diary
of
1/5th N. Lan. R.
for the period
June 1st to June 30th, 1917.

Army Form C. 2118

# WAR DIARY
## or
## INTELLIGENCE SUMMARY
*(Erase heading not required.)*

| Place | Date | Hour | Summary of Events and Information | Remarks and references to Appendices |
|---|---|---|---|---|
| | 1/6/17. | | RAILWAY WOOD. Battalion as "Support Working Battalion". Dispositions as under:- <br> "B" Coy. - ECOLE <br> "C" " - ST. JAMES' TRENCH - 1 platoon. <br> POTIJZE - 1 platoon. <br> "A" " - HALF MOON TRENCH - 1 platoon. <br> "D" " - HEDGE TRENCH - 1 platoon. <br> SOUTH LANE - 2 platoons. <br> H.Q. " - <br> 4 Lewis Guns and teams attached to 1/5th S.Lan.R. in Front line. <br> Gas discharge against enemy on our front at 3-0 a.m. | |
| | 2/6/17. | | Another discharge of gas on our front against enemy at 3-0 a.m. Practice barrage commenced at 3-30 p.m. and continued for half an hour. <br> Casualties :- 1 O.R. wounded. | |
| | 3/6/17. | | Bombardment and Barrage on whole of Second Army front, accompanied by discharge of Smoke bombs from 2.0 to 3.30pm. Enemy heavy Artillery very active all night. Dump fired near HELL FIRE CORNER, culminating in terrific explosion. Heavy discharge of Gas Shells causing much inconvenience to Transport coming up with rations about midnight. H.Q. was fairly clear, but outlying Companies forced to don Box Respirators. 4 O.R. wounded <br> Casualties :- 3 O.R. killed. 1 O.R. missing. <br> 14 Horses gassed. | |
| | 4/6/17. | | Casualty :- 1 O.R. wounded. | |
| | 5/6/17. | | Battalion moved to take up line as left Battalion of right Brigade, relieving 1 Company 5th South Lancs. Regt., in front line and 1 Company 10th Scottish R.R. in POTIJZE. | |

**Army Form C. 2118**

# WAR DIARY
## or
## INTELLIGENCE SUMMARY
*(Erase heading not required.)*

Instructions regarding War Diaries and Intelligence Summaries are contained in F. S. Regs., Part II. and the Staff Manual respectively. Title Pages will be prepared in manuscript.

| Place | Date | Hour | Summary of Events and Information | Remarks and references to Appendices |
|---|---|---|---|---|
| | 5/6/17. | | Contd. Dispositions:- "A" Company remained in HALF MOON TRENCH. "B" " ST JAMES TRENCH 1 Platoon, POTIJZE REDOUBT 1 Platoon POTIJZE 1 Platoon. "C" " Front Line. "D" " POTIJZE. Headquarters, DRAGOON FARM. | |
| | 6/6/17. | | 2/Lieut. Humphrey joined Battalion for Duty, from England. Casualty:- 1 O.R. wounded. | |
| | 7/6/17. | | Second Army attacked at 5.10 a.m. from South of YPRES salient to PLOEG STEERT. Mine blown and artillery 5.10 a.m. O.C. "C" Coy. sent out two fighting patrols in conjunction with companies on right and left to ascertain if and how the enemy trenches were held. Report:- Held strongly. | |
| | 8/6/17. | | Patrols again sent out for same purpose as last night and with similar result. 2/Lieut. Hamilton rejoined from hospital, 9.6.17 Casualties:- 4 O.R. wounded. | |
| | 9/6/17. | | XIX Corps Commander sent message of appreciation and thanks to 166 Brigade for good work done during the preceding few days. 2/Lieut. Woods joined Battalion for Duty from R.F.C. | |
| | 10/6/17. | | Enemy used Gas Shells extensively on YPRES and MENIN ROAD causing great inconvenience to transport. | |
| | 11/6/17. | | "A" Coy. relieved "C" in Front Line. General P. De la Gough visited trenches along with Divisional General. | |

Army Form C. 2118.

# WAR DIARY
## or
## INTELLIGENCE SUMMARY.
*(Erase heading not required.)*

Instructions regarding War Diaries and Intelligence Summaries are contained in F. S. Regs., Part II. and the Staff Manual respectively. Title pages will be prepared in manuscript.

| Place | Date | Hour | Summary of Events and Information | Remarks and references to Appendices |
|---|---|---|---|---|
| | 12/6/17. | | Small mine blown by British in Railway Wood Sector, later enemy blew 5 counter mines. | |
| | 15/6/17. | | 55th Division transferred to Fifth Army. | |
| | 15/6/17. | | Headquarters transferred from DRAGOON FARM to SOUTH LANE. | |
| | 16/6/17. | | Casualties:- 3 O.R. wounded. (including 1 at duty). 1 O.R. " Died of wounds 17/6/17. | |
| | 17/6/17. | | "B" Coy. relieved "A" Coy. in Front Line. "A" Coy. moved to HALF MOON TRENCH. Casualty: 1 O.R. wounded. | |
| | 18/6/17. | | Headquarters moved to HALF MOON TRENCH. "A" Coy. " " SOUTH LANE. "D" " " HEDGE TRENCH. Casualties:- 3 O.R. wounded including 3 at duty. 1 O.R. " Died of wounds 19.6.17. | |
| | 19/6/17. | | Casualties:- 3 O.R. wounded 2 at Duty. | |
| | 20/6/17. | | Casualties:- 4 O.R. killed in action. 1 O.R. wounded. Died of wounds 22.6.17. 2 O.R. " including 1 at Duty. 1 O.R. " (Carrying Coy. attd. 177 Tunnels. Coy.) Battalion relieved by 7th/8th K.O.S.B. in RAILWAY WOOD Sector relief complete 1 a.m. Battalion proceeded to DERBY CAMP (H.1.c.8.9.) | |
| | 22/6/17. | | Battalion marched from DERBY CAMP at 9 a.m. to POPERINGHE Main Station, entraining at 11.30 a.m. Detrained ST OMER at 4.30 p.m. and marched to billets at LOQUIN arriving | |

Army Form C. 2118

# WAR DIARY
## or
## INTELLIGENCE SUMMARY

*(Erase heading not required.)*

Instructions regarding War Diaries and Intelligence Summaries are contained in F. S. Regs., Part II. and the Staff Manual respectively. Title Pages will be prepared in manuscript.

| Place | Date | Hour | Summary of Events and Information | Remarks and references to Appendices |
|---|---|---|---|---|
| | 23/6/17. | | ACQUIN V.16 - V.21. - V.22. Reference map FRANCE No.27a S.E. Cleaning up generally and kit inspections. | |
| | 24/6/17. to 30/6/17. | | Training at ACQUIN. | |

Lieut. Colonel.

Cmdg. 1/5th Loyal North Lancs. Regt.

Army Form C. 2118.

1/5th Royal Lancashire Regt.

# WAR DIARY
## INTELLIGENCE SUMMARY
*(Erase heading not required.)*

| Place | Date | Hour | Summary of Events and Information | Remarks and references to Appendices |
|---|---|---|---|---|
| ACQUIN V.16.-V.21.- V.22. Ref map FRANCE 1:27,000 S.E. | 1/7/17 to 5/7/17 | | Training at ACQUIN, and Special Brigade Drawing. | |
| | 6/7/17 | | Moved from billets in ACQUIN to billets in SETQUES (about 4 miles SE of ACQUIN) | |
| SETQUES | 7/7/17 | | Brigade Practice attack on German trenches – Tanks co-operating (other rank accidentally wounded) | |
| | 8/7/17 | | Church Parade. | |
| | 9/7/17 | | Battalion training. | |
| | 10/7/17 to 12/7/17 | | | |
| | 13/7/17 | | Brigade Practice in semi-open warfare. 1 other rank gravel, able (wounded) (attd. Trench Mortar (PRES) | |
| | 14/7/17 | | Brigade Practice attack on German trenches. | |
| | 15/7/17 | | Brigade Sports day at OUVE LME Sq. | |
| | 16/7/17 | | Battalion training | |
| | 17/7/17 | | – do – | |
| | 17/18/7/17 | | Final rehearsal of Brigade attack on German trenches at Dawn 18/7/17. | |

1/5th Royal Warwickshire Regt.

Army Form C. 2118.

# WAR DIARY
# INTELLIGENCE SUMMARY.
(Erase heading not required.)

| Place | Date | Hour | Summary of Events and Information | Remarks and references to Appendices |
|---|---|---|---|---|
| SETQUES | 19/7/17 | | Battalion training | |
| | 20/7/17 | | Battalion left SETQUES by route march to ST. OMER. Entrained ST. OMER at 11-0 a.m. detrained POPERINGHE at 2-30 p.m., proceeding by route march to QUERY CAMP, nr VLAMERTINGHE. | |
| QUERY CAMP | 21/7/17 | | Provided parties to work in the forward area. Casualty — 1 other rank wounded | |
| | 22/7/17 | | Provided parties to work in forward area. - Casualty 1 other rank wounded | |
| | 23/7/17 | | do — Casualty 2/Lt D.S. Hamilton wounded | |
| WIELTJE | 24/7/17 | | Relieved 1/10th (Scottish) Bn. King's L'pool Regt in the WIELTJE Sector. Relief complete 10-30 p.m. — 3 Coys in the Line — "C" Company at DERBY (CAMP) Casualties — 4 other ranks wounded including 1 at duty | |
| | 25/7/17 | | Casualties — 2 other ranks killed — 19 wounded - including 7 at duty and 1 Died of wounds | |
| | 26/7/17 | | Casualties — 5 other ranks wounded including 1 at duty | |
| | 27/7/17 | | "B" Company withdrawn from line to GOLDFISH CHATEAU in L4 Area. Our Artillery carried out numerous bombardments of enemy trench systems. Casualties — 4 other ranks killed = 2/Lt P.O. DAVIES wounded at duty = 11 other ranks wounded - including 5 at duty, and 1 Died of wounds |  |

2353  Wt. W2514/1454  700,000  5/15  D. D. & L.  A.D.S.S./Forms/C. 2118.

Army Form C. 2118.

1/5th Loyal North Lancashire Regt.

# WAR DIARY
or
# INTELLIGENCE SUMMARY.
(Erase heading not required.)

Instructions regarding War Diaries and Intelligence Summaries are contained in F.S. Regs., Part II. and the Staff Manual respectively. Title pages will be prepared in manuscript.

| Place | Date | Hour | Summary of Events and Information | Remarks and references to Appendices |
|---|---|---|---|---|
| WIELTJE | 28/7/17 | | "C" Company relieved "A" Company in BILGE TRENCH. Our Artillery continued bombardment of enemy trench system. Party consisting of 1 Officer (2/Lt TIFFEN WOOD) 5 N.C.Os. and 30 other ranks attacked enemy trenches between C.29.a 26.10 and C.29.a.45.65 at 5.15 a.m. approximately. 1 of the enemy taken prisoner and about 20 of the enemy killed. 1 dug-out containing bodies blown up. Casualties — 1 other rank killed — 2/Lt F.F. WOOD wounded — 4 other ranks wounded. | |
| | 29/7 | | "B" Company took over LIVERPOOL TRENCH. Our Artillery heavily bombarded enemy trenches and communications during day and night. Casualties — 5 other ranks killed — 5 other ranks wounded — including 3 at Duty. | |
| | 30/7/17 | | Our Artillery again heavily bombarded enemy trenches and communications during day and night. Casualties — 2/Lt J. KENNEDY wounded. 9 other ranks wounded. | |

1/5th Loyal North Lancs Regt.

# WAR DIARY
## INTELLIGENCE SUMMARY

Army Form C. 2118.

| Place | Date | Hour | Summary of Events and Information | Remarks and references to Appendices |
|---|---|---|---|---|
| WIELTJE | 31/7/17 | | Casualties:- | |
| | | | Killed - Lieut. (A/Capt). H. CHRONNELL | |
| | | | Lieut. G. GLAISTER. | |
| | | | Lieut. J. S. CARR. | |
| | | | | |
| | | | Wounded - Lt. Col. T. O. SMITH | |
| | | | Lieut (A/Capt) S. L. REDFERN. | |
| | | | 2/Lt. M. H. TUTT. | |
| | | | R. T. THORNLEY. | |
| | | | J. M. WOODS | |
| | | | | |
| | | | Approximate total of casualties - other ranks, 150. | |
| | | | | |
| | | | List of Officers who took part in the Operation:- | |
| | | | Lieut Col. T. O. Smith. Capt. A. Entwistle, Capt. W. Long, Capt. H. Chronnell | |
| | | | Capt. S. L. Redfern, Capt. R. W. B. Sparkes, Lieut G. Glaister, | |
| | | | Lieut J. S. Carr, 2/Lt. S. J. Curtis, 2/Lt. L. B. Wray, 2/Lt. J. J. Walker | |
| | | | 2/Lt. J. Faulkner, 2/Lt. R. T. Thornley, 2/Lt. W. Marsden, 2/Lt. L. H. Humphrey | |
| | | | 2/Lt. D. S. Hamilton (attached Brigade carrying Party) 2/Lt. b. A. Robertson | |
| | | | (8th Manchester Regt attd) 2/Lt. P. O. Dawes (4th R.W.F. attd) 2/Lt. J. A. Jones (4th R.W.F. attd)(sick to Brigade) | |
| | | | 2/Lt. J. M. H. Tutt (3rd L.N Fus R. attd). Lt. J. A. Jones (4th R W Fus attd)(in Jamison Off.) | |
| | | | Lt. Long, Captain for Major | |
| | | | Lomaly 1/5 th Loyal N. Lancs R. | |

1/5 K. Royal North Lancs. Regt.

Army Form C. 2118

WAR DIARY
or
INTELLIGENCE SUMMARY
(Erase heading not required.)

| Place | Date | Hour | Summary of Events and Information | Remarks and references to Appendices |
|---|---|---|---|---|
| WIELTJE | 31/7/17 | | 4th Afk Army attacked German trench system along the whole of its front at ZERO = 3-50 a.m. 1/5th Loyal North Lancashire Regt. attacked German trenches on a front of 350 yds. penetrating 400 yds beyond enemy third line. "A" and "B" companies gained the Battalion's first objective and "C" and "D" companies reached second objective as per programme. Numerous prisoners being taken. The 166th Infantry Brigade objective was reached in the allotted time and finally the 55th Division objective was gained, i.e. the GREEN LINE. Later during the afternoon the Germans counter-attacked on the front [line?] of the 55th Division and our line was withdrawn to the BLACK LINE. 1/5th K.R. Lancs Regt. moving up to support 1/10th (Scottish) Kings L'pool Regt. and 1/5th South Lancs Regt. , 1/5th Kings Own (R.L.R.) moving up and occupying whole of BLUELINE. Order of Battle for Attack. On our right 1/5th Kings Own (R.L.R.), on our left 12th Suffolk Regt., 39th Division. | |

Vol 24

166/55

War Diary
of the
1/5 N. Lan. R.
for the period
1st July to 31st July,
1917.

Vol 25

166/55

War Diary

of

1/5th N. Lan. R.

for period

1st to 31st August, 1917.

1/5th Royal North Lancashire Regt.

**WAR DIARY**
or
**INTELLIGENCE SUMMARY.**
(Erase heading not required.)

Army Form C. 2118.

| Place | Date | Hour | Summary of Events and Information | Remarks and references to Appendices |
|---|---|---|---|---|
| TRENCHES C.23.c BELGIUM Sheet 28 NW. | 1/8/17 | | Germans heavily shelled our positions in trenches throughout the day. The ground became a complete quagmire through incessant rain. Casualties - 3 other ranks killed. 12 other ranks wounded. | |
| WIELTJE Defences. C.22.b BELGIUM Sheet 28 NW | 2/8/17 | | Germans heavily shelled our positions finalises during the day. Relieved by 13th Royal Irish Rifles (36th Division) in front line system. Battalion took up positions in WIELTJE DEFENCES. Casualties - 1 other ranks killed. 24 other ranks wounded. | |
| | 3/8/17 | | Battalion relieved in WIELTJE DEFENCES by 14th Royal Irish Rifles (36th Division) and proceeded by platoons to camp near VLAMERTINGHE, H.9.c. Sheet 28 N.W. Casualties - 1 other rank killed. 7 other ranks wounded, including 1 at duty. | |
| CAMP near WATOU | 4/8/17 | | Battalion entrained at VLAMERTINGHE at 7.0 a.m., detrained POPERINGHE at 7.45 a.m. and marched to camp near WATOU, arriving in camp about 11.0 a.m. | |
| | 6/8/17 | | Battalion paraded on Camp Parade Ground at 7 a.m. and marched to ABEELE. Entrained ABEELE at 8 a.m., detrained AUDRUICQ | |

1/5th Royal North Lancashire Regt.

# WAR DIARY
## or
## INTELLIGENCE SUMMARY.
*(Erase heading not required.)*

Army Form C. 2118.

| Place | Date | Hour | Summary of Events and Information | Remarks and references to Appendices |
|---|---|---|---|---|
| RECQUES J.10.c and d. Sheet 27 NE FRANCE | 6/8/17 | | at 4-0 a.m. 7-8-17. Thence by motor lorries to billets in RECQUES J.10.c and d., FRANCE Sheet 27 NE. | |
| | 7/8/17 | | Cleaning up and kit inspections | |
| | 8/8/17 to 31/8/17 | | Company, Battalion and Brigade training | |

A. Long. Captain
I/R Col. Comdg. 1/5 N. Lan R.

166/55

Vol 26

War Diary
of the
1/5 M'Rank
1st Hunroos
1st to 30th September 1917

# WAR DIARY
## INTELLIGENCE SUMMARY.
*(Erase heading not required.)*

Army Form C. 2118.

| Place | Date | Hour | Summary of Events and Information | Remarks and references to Appendices |
|---|---|---|---|---|
| RECQUES J.10.C&D SHEET 27NE FRANCE | 1.9.14 to 12.9.14 | | Bugacle, Battalion and Company training. | |
| | 13.9.14 | | Battalion left RECQUES at 2:30am by route march to AUDRUICQ. Entrained AUDRUICQ 11.0 am, detrained VLAMERTINGHE at 6.30pm. Bivouced in field near GOLDFISH CHATEAU for the night. | |
| CANAL BANK YPRES. | 14.9.14 | | Moved to dugouts on Canal Bank, YPRES, in the afternoon. Supplied working parties to 164th Infantry Brigade in front and support system. | |
| | 15.9.14 to 12.9.14 | | Supplied working parties for 164th Infantry Brigade in front and support system. | |
| | 16.9.14 | | Casualties:- WOUNDED 2/Lt. T.A. JONES (att. R.W.Fs. attd.) Capt. B.H. MAKANT (att. 1/4 L.F.) 1 9th Rank. KILLED 2 Other Ranks. | |
| | 17.9.14 | | -do- KILLED 1 Other Rank. WOUNDED 7 other Ranks, including 1 self-inflicted and 1 Shell Shock. | |
| | 18.9.14 | | -do- WOUNDED 3 Other Ranks. | |

# WAR DIARY
## or
## INTELLIGENCE SUMMARY.
*(Erase heading not required.)*

Army Form C. 2118.

Instructions regarding War Diaries and Intelligence Summaries are contained in F. S. Regs., Part II. and the Staff Manual respectively. Title pages will be prepared in manuscript.

| Place | Date | Hour | Summary of Events and Information | Remarks and references to Appendices |
|---|---|---|---|---|
| | 19.9.17 | | Battalion attached to 165 Infantry Bde. moved from Canal Bank via Ypres to German pill-box WIELTJE, Completing move by 2.30am 20th Sept. Batt. H.Q. at UHLAN FARM. | |
| | 20.9.17 | | 55th Div. attacked Jacob's craft at ST JULIEN. 5th L.N. Lan. R. Pattacked to 165 supported by 10th Lpool Scots. Battalion took part in Brigade assault on the objective of HILL 37. Bere machine gunned in afternoon counter-attack on Hill 37. | |
| | 21.9.17 22.9.17 | | Consolidated the ground gained and held for Brigade. Shelling on both days very heavy. (53rd Divn) and came back by hosts to bivouac near GOLDFISH CHATEAU, VLAMERTINGHE arriving early morning 23rd. KILLED 20 other Ranks. WOUNDED 2/Lt S. CURTIS, 2/Lt R.C. DAVIES, 2/Lt T. HOWARD, 2/Lt F. RUTHERFORD (at duty) 140 other Ranks. MISSING 2/Lt G.H. NEWHA, 3 other Ranks. | |
| WATOU 23.9.17 No. 2 Area | | | Battalion moved from VLAMERTINGHE at 9am by Motor Buses to WATOU No.2 area. | |

Army Form C. 2118.

# WAR DIARY
## or
## INTELLIGENCE SUMMARY.
*(Erase heading not required.)*

Instructions regarding War Diaries and Intelligence Summaries are contained in F. S. Regs., Part II. and the Staff Manual respectively. Title pages will be prepared in manuscript.

| Place | Date | Hour | Summary of Events and Information | Remarks and references to Appendices |
|---|---|---|---|---|
| | 26/9/17 | | Brigadier General & 3 officers addressed Bn's and complimented them on their splendid achievements during the operations 20th & 27th Sept. Bn. later marched out to cross-country trip from Ring Farm Camp to 166 Inf. Brigade. Battalion paraded at Ref. Farm, WATOU. Bn. then entrained. Marched | |
| BEAULENCOURT M.M. FRANCE | | | via POPERINGHE (SWITCH ROAD) to PROVEN. Entrained PROVEN Railway Siding | |
| | | | MIRAUMONT to BAPAUME 7.30 p.m. and marched by route to Camp near | |
| | | | BEAULENCOURT Area, arriving there at 12 midnight. | |
| | 31/9/17 28/9/17 | | Company training | |
| | | | Battalion provided road party. Le TRANSLOY | |
| LONGAVESNES 29/9/17 | | | Brigade via ROCQUIGNY, LE MESNIL, MANANCOURT, NURLU, AIZECOURT, to camp at LONGAVESNES arriving there at 4.30 p.m. dinners very shortly en route. Brigadier inspected Battalion on its march. | |
| TRENCHES 30/9/17 Ref. Map TRENCH MAPS 1/10,000 57c HQ X15.c.80 to East From X 14 Central To X 10.6.92.60 | | | Bn. marched on foot from VILLERS FAUCON at 10 a.m. and arrived in front line system of trenches relieving 1/4th Bn. Gloucest. Regt. opposite VILLERS FAUCON and EPEHY. Relief complete 10 pm. | Disposition: A Royal line B Royal Sup. C Royal Res. S. Coy. front line Coy HQ 1/5 'B' Royal Sup. Btn. |

(A7883) D. D. & L. London, E.C. Wt. W809/M1672 359,000 4/17 Sch. 52a Forms/C/2118/14

War Diary
of the
15th Hussars
for the period
1st to 31st October 1917.

Vol 27

Army Form C. 2118.

1/5th Loyal N. Lancs. Regt.
WAR DIARY
~~INTELLIGENCE SUMMARY~~
(Erase heading not required.)

Instructions regarding War Diaries and Intelligence Summaries are contained in F. S. Regs., Part II. and the Staff Manual respectively. Title pages will be prepared in manuscript.

| Place | Date | Hour | Summary of Events and Information | Remarks and references to Appendices |
|---|---|---|---|---|
| TRENCHES HONNECOURT Left Sub-Sector. Ref.Map FRANCE Sheet 57c SE.1/20000. X.17.b.00.20. to X.11.a.20.70. | 1/10/17. to 3/10/17. | | Dispositions of Companies:- <br> "B" Coy. - Right front. <br> "D" " - Left " <br> "C" " - Support. <br> "A" " - Reserve. | |
| | 4/10/17. | | 2/Lt. H.N.Hobson (3rd N.Lan.R.) joined Bn. for duty from England. | |
| | 6/10/17. | | Inter-Coy. relief. <br> New dispositions as under :- <br> "A" Coy. - Right front. <br> "C" " - Left " <br> "D" " - Support. <br> "B" " - Reserve. | |
| LONGAVESNES. Ref.Map FRANCE Sheet 62c 1/40,000, E.25.b. | 13/10/17. | | Battalion relieved by 1/5th Bn. "The King's" L'pool Regt. and marched independently by Companies to LONGAVESNES via VILLERS GUISLAIN - EPEHY - ST.EMILIE - VILLERS FAUCON. Relief complete 11-0 p.m. No casualties were sustained during the whole period Bn. was in the trenches. | |
| | 14/10/17. | | Cleaning up generally and kit inspections. Capt. F.K.Mallett transferred to ENGLAND for 6 months duty with a Home Battalion. | |
| | 15/10/17. | | Platoon and Company Training. <br> 2/Lt. A.Fraser <br> " E.L.Hall } (3rd N.Lan.R.) joined Bn.for duty <br> " E.N.O.Weighill } from England. | |

Army Form C. 2118.

# 1/5th Loyal North Lancs. Regt.
## WAR DIARY
### INTELLIGENCE SUMMARY.

*(Erase heading not required.)*

Instructions regarding War Diaries and Intelligence Summaries are contained in F. S. Regs., Part II. and the Staff Manual respectively. Title pages will be prepared in manuscript.

| Place | Date | Hour | Summary of Events and Information | Remarks and references to Appendices |
|---|---|---|---|---|
| | 16/10/17 to 18/10/17. | | Platoon and Company Training. On 18/10/17 Maj.Gen.Wright witnessed Instructional | |
| | 19/10/17. | | Platoon of Officers and N.C.O's. in attack. 166 Infantry Brigade paraded at LONGAVESNES at 10-0 a.m. for inspection by Major General Wright of the United States Army. | |
| | 20/10/17. | | Major General Wright, United States Army witnessed practise attack on enemy trenches carried out by 166 Infantry Brigade at LONGAVESNES. 2/Lt. J.Rankin ) <br> " C.B.Cowan ) <br> " J.S.Smith ) (3rd N.Lan.R.) joined Bn. for duty from <br> " T.A.Barter ) England. <br> " A.B.Robson ) | |
| | 21/10/17. | | Church Parade and inspections. | |
| | 22/10/17. | | Platoon and Company Training. <br> 2/Lt. W.B.Leigh )(3rd N.Lan.R.) joined Bn. for duty from <br> " C.A.Bryan ) England. | |
| Trenches HONNECOURT Ref.Map FRANCE Sht.57c SE. X.17.b.00.20. to X.11.a.20.70. | 23/10/17. | | Relieved 1/5th Bn. "The King's" L'Pool. Regt. in HONNECOURT Sub-sector. Relief complete 10-30 p.m. <br> Dispositions :- <br> "B" Coy. - Right front. <br> "D" " - Left " <br> "A" " - Support. <br> "C" " - Reserve. | |
| | 27/10/17. | | 600 gas projectiles discharged against enemy line at 3-0 a.m. Very little retaliation by enemy. | |
| | 28/10/17. | | Inter-Company relief. <br> New dispositions as overleaf:- | |

Army Form C. 2118.

# 1/5th Loyal North Lancs. Regt. WAR DIARY or ~~INTELLIGENCE SUMMARY~~

(Erase heading not required.)

Instructions regarding War Diaries and Intelligence Summaries are contained in F. S. Regs., Part II. and the Staff Manual respectively. Title pages will be prepared in manuscript.

| Place | Date | Hour | Summary of Events and Information | Remarks and references to Appendices |
|---|---|---|---|---|
| TRENCHES. | 28/10/17 (cont.) | | "A" Coy. - Right front. <br> "C" " - Left " <br> "B" " - Support. <br> "D" " - Reserve. <br> Capt. A.W.Jones proceeded to H.Q., Royal Flying Corps for attachment as observer. | |

W. Chadwick Major
Cmdg. 1/5th Loyal North Lancs. Regt.

166/55

9/11/28

War of the
1st Regiment
for the Funeral
1st to 30th November
1917

Army Form C. 2118.

# WAR DIARY
## or
## INTELLIGENCE SUMMARY

(Erase heading not required.)

Instructions regarding War Diaries and Intelligence Summaries are contained in F. S. Regs., Part II. and the Staff Manual respectively. Title Pages will be prepared in manuscript.

| Place | Date | Hour | Summary of Events and Information | Remarks and references to Appendices |
|---|---|---|---|---|
| Trenches HONNECOURT CENTRE SUB-SECTOR | 1/11/17 | | Relieved by 1/5th R. South Lancs. Regt. and proceeded to Brigade Reserve. DISPOSITIONS :- BATTN. H.Q.; 'A' Coy & C' Coy — VAUCELLETTE FARM. 'B' Company 2 Platoons — LIMERICK POST. " D " 2 " — KILDARE POST. — MEATH POST. | |
| VAUCELLETTE FM. | 2/11/17 | | Cleaning up etc. | |
| | 3/11/17 | | Provided Working Parties and Improving Dugouts. | |
| | 4/11/17 | | Raid Party practised for Raid on HONNECOURT WOOD. | |
| | 5/11/17 | | Provided Working Parties. | |
| | 6/11/17 | | Do. | |
| | 7/11/17 to 9/11/17 | | Do. | |
| TRENCHES HONNECOURT CENTRE SUB-SECTOR | 10/11/17 | | Relieved 1/5" South Lancs. Regt. Casualties 1 Other Rank. AT DUTY. | |
| | 11/11/17 | | DISPOSITIONS :- 'A' Coy — Right Front; 'C' Coy - Left Front. 'B' - Support; 'D' - Reserve. 'A' Coy reconnoitring Patrol encountered large German Patrol went out twice. Flare to Light Enemy turned out. Patrol managed to send out twice. A German stretcher was recovered to save his line next morning. Casualties 1 Other Rank Killed, 1 Other Rank Wounded. | |
| | 12/11/17 | | 'C' & 'D' Coys carried out Raid on HONNECOURT WOOD, (Residenous) 2/Lt. Kilbourne + Artison divided into 3 Parties, RED, BLUE & WHITE. Preliminary bombardment successful and Parties reached enemy wire. 2nd Bangalore torpedo failed to explode. Party returned without achieving their object. Casualties 2 Other Ranks Wounded. | |

# WAR DIARY
## INTELLIGENCE SUMMARY

*(Erase heading not required.)*

Army Form C. 2118.

Instructions regarding War Diaries and Intelligence Summaries are contained in F. S. Regs., Part II. and the Staff Manual respectively. Title Pages will be prepared in manuscript.

| Place | Date | Hour | Summary of Events and Information | Remarks and references to Appendices |
|---|---|---|---|---|
| | 15/11/17 | | Inter Company Reliefs :- 'B' relieved 'A' Coy - Right Front, 'D' Coy relieved 'C' Coy - Left Front, 'C' Coy - Support, 'A' Coy - Reserve. | |
| | 19/11/17 | | Casualties 2 other Ranks Wounded, including 1 O.R. at Duty. | |
| | 20/11/17 | 6.30am | Heavy bombardment opened followed by attack by British troops. Divisions on left, i.e. 12th, formed Right flank of attack which extended over about front of about 5 miles. Attack highly successful. At the same time the Infantry Brigade carried out attack on GILLEMONT FARM and the KNOLL — after holding in the German Front trenches at GILLEMONT FARM for a few hours they withdrew to original line. Casualties :- 1 O.R. Killed, Right enemy shelling of TAWCUS AVENUE. 2 O.R. Wounded. | |
| | | | Inter Coy Reliefs :- 'A' Coy relieved 'B' Coy - Right Front, 'C' Coy relieved 'D' Coy Left Front, 'D' Coy Support, 'B' Coy - Reserve. | |
| | 21/11/17 | | Increased Enemy On activity. Casualties 1 O.R. Wounded. | |
| | | | TAWCUS AVENUE intermittently shelled. | |
| | 22/11/17 | | Inter Company Reliefs :- 'B' Coy relieved 'A' Coy - Right Front, 'D' Coy relieved 'C' Coy - Left Front, 'A' Coy - Support, 'C' Coy - Reserve. | |
| | 24/11/17 | | | |
| | 26/11/17 | | Enemy Shell Front line: STORAR AV, GLOSTER RD, and LEITH WALM. | |
| | 28/11/17 | | | |
| | 29/11/17 | | Freshen shell front line and GLOSTER RD, at intervals during day. So steep heavy German bombardment along whole of front followed by strong attack. Front line Coys. overrun, noting capable of stopping tank exactly happened. Enemy seen approaching GLOSTER RD. from direction known as what in great numbers at about 9am. BATT. H.Q. made stand in GLOSTER RD. | SHERWOOD LT. |
| | 30/11/17 | | | |

2449 Wt. W14957/M90 750,000 1/16 J.B.C. & A. Forms/C.2118/12.

3

## WAR DIARY.

| Place | Date | Hour | Summary of Events and Information | Reference to Appendices and Remarks |
|---|---|---|---|---|
| | 30/11/17 | | until 8.30 a.m. Enemy themselves outflanked on both sides by the enemy they were forced to withdraw to fourteen Willows where they dug in. 3 Officers Wounded. 2 Officers Wounded & Missing, 16 Officers Missing. 2 O.R. Killed, 27 O.R. Wounded. 384 Other Ranks Missing. | |

R.W.R. Parks Capt.
Comdg. 15th Tyne N. Lan. Regt.

Vol 29

War Diary
of the
1/5th R.Lan.R.
for the period
1st to 31st December 1917.

Army Form C. 2118.

# WAR DIARY
## ~~INTELLIGENCE SUMMARY~~
*(Erase heading not required.)*

Instructions regarding War Diaries and Intelligence Summaries are contained in F.S. Regs., Part II. and the Staff Manual respectively. Title pages will be prepared in manuscript.

| Place | Date | Hour | Summary of Events and Information | Remarks and references to Appendices |
|---|---|---|---|---|
| 14 Willows | 1.12.17 | | Digging in and constructing new line at Fourteen Willows. | |
| VILLERS-GUISLAIN 10,000 SE.4. (Nroman) | 2.12.17 | | Battn. held line about 400 yards in front of VAUGHANS BANK. Relieved on the night of 4th-5th Dec. by 9th Leicester Regt., 21st Division Battn. | |
| BUIRE | 3.12.17 | | Proceeded to BUIRE. | |
| | 4.12.17 | | Cleaning up. etc. | |
| | 5.12.17 | | Do. | |
| FLAMICOURT | 6.12.17 | | Proceeded by march route from BUIRE to FLAMICOURT — PERONNE. Rested at FLAMICOURT. Draft of 18 joined Battn. from 55th Divnl. Reinforcement Depot Battn. | |
| | 7.12.17 | | Remained at FLAMICOURT. 2 Officers joined Battn. | |
| | 8.12.17 | | A draft of 20 O.R. joined Battn. from 55th Divl. R.D. Battn. | |
| NOYELLE AVION | 9.12.17 | | Battn. proceeded by train to AUBIGNY, where it detrained about 5 p.m. and continued by march route to NOYELLE AVION. The Battn. was accommodated in huts. | |
| | 10.12.17 | | Battn. rested at NOYELLE. | |
| CHELERS | 11.12.17 | | Do. Moved by march to CHELERS where Battn. rested in billets. Draft of 25 O.R. joined Battn. 2 Officers of R'igo. Rovn. also joined. | |
| TROISVAUX | 12.12.17 | | Moved by march route to TROISVAUX, the Divisional Band leading the column. The men rested in billets. 4 Officers joined the Battn. from 1st to. Liv. Regt. | |

A 5834  Wt.W4973/M687. 750,000 8/16 D.D.& L. Ltd. Forms/C.2118/13.

Army Form C. 2118.

# WAR DIARY

## INTELLIGENCE SUMMARY

(Erase heading not required.)

Instructions regarding War Diaries and Intelligence Summaries are contained in F. S. Regs., Part II. and the Staff Manual respectively. Title pages will be prepared in manuscript.

| Place | Date | Hour | Summary of Events and Information | Remarks and references to Appendices |
|---|---|---|---|---|
| FONTAINE LES BOURLANS | 13/12/17 | | Battn. moved by march route to FONTAINE LES BOURLANS. Men rested in billets. | |
| | 14.12.17 | | Do. Battalion accommodated in billets | |
| ERNY ST JULIEN | 15.12.17 | | Do. ERNY ST JULIEN. - | |
| | 16.12.17 | | Day devoted to cleaning up, re-equipping &c - 32 O.R. joined Battn from 55th Divisional Reinforcement Depot. Rifle and Bros. | |
| | 17.12.17 | | Cleaning up &c. 3 Officers of South Lancs. Regt. joined from England. Brig-Gen. KENTISH D.S.O. took command of Demonstration Platoon, picked from the Battn. 11 Officers of South Lancashire Regt. joined Battn from England | |
| | 18.12.17 | | Brig Genl KENTISH addressed all N.C.Os of Battn. who taking over command of 116th Bagde. took Demonstration Platoon during morning. The Divisional Commander also addressed the Officers and N.C.Os of the Brigade on the situation. 8 Officer of South Lancs joined from England. | |
| | 19.12.17 | | Platoon gave demonstration under the direction of Brigade Commander, to who addressed all Ranks of the Brigade on tanks, followed by an address by Brig-Gen. JEUDWINE | |
| | 20.12.17 | | Battn. engaged in Platoon and Company training - one day ie musketry. | |
| | 21.12.17 | | General training carried on. | |
| | 22.12.17 | | Draft of 127 O.R. joined Battn from 55th Div. Reinforcement Depot Battn. Continuation of general training. | |
| | 23.12.17 | | Do. 2 Officers S.W. Lancs. joined Battn. from 3rd S.W. Lancs | |
| | 24.12.17 | | Do. | |
| | 25.12.17 | | Christmas Day. Decorum. Seeing ametieon in the evening | |

# WAR DIARY

Army Form C. 2118.

| Place | Date | Hour | Summary of Events and Information | Remarks and references to Appendices |
|---|---|---|---|---|
| ERNY ST JULIEN. | 26.12.17 | | Boxing Day. The weather remained severe with snow. | |
| | 27.12.17 | | 3 Officers of Loyal North Lancs Regt. joined from 8th L.N.R Regt. General training of the Battn proceeded with. | |
| | 28.12.17 | | Demonstration Company of 4 platoons paraded before the officers + N.C.Os of the Brigade at 10 a.m. on "AINTREE RACE COURSE", BOMY. | |
| | 29.12.17 | | General training continued. B Coy on firing range. | |
| | 30.12.17 | | Church parade in morning. | |
| | 31.12.17 | | General training. Bombing practice by Coys. | |

1/16

J Aubleur Lt
for Lt Col
Comdg 1/5th L N LAN R

166/55
Vol 30

War Diary
of the
1/5th N. Han. R.
for the period
1st to 31st January
1918.

ARMY FORM C 2118

H.Q.
166TH INFANTRY BDE.
No. ......................
Date. ......................

1/5 Loyal North Lancs Regt

War Diary - Janvary 1918

ERNY ST JULIEN.

| | |
|---|---|
| 1-1-18 | Training Programme for day carried. 1 officer and 60 OR joined Battn |
| 2-1-18 | Battalion on the range under Capt Mayers. Lieut Col Anderson assumes command of Battalion. 3 Officers joined Battalion |
| 3-1-18 | Battalion less D Coy and specialist Class paraded in close column of Coys in fighting order. Demonstration by C O & Officers & NCOs of Coy in attack. D Coy on Range for Musketry and rapid wiring. |
| 4-1-18 | Coys cleaning up site from 9AM - 10-30 AM. 10-45 AM. Battalion parade close column of Coys for Brigade day on Arctic Pacceura |
| 5-1-18. | Rifle competition carried out by Coys. |
| 6-1-18 | Draft of 15 ORs and 1 Officer joined Battn from 55 DRDB. Church Parade held |
| 7-1-18 | A.C.D Coys carried out training in Winter Pacceurus. Officers parade for tactical exercise under the C.O. B Coy in Range. |
| 8-1-18 | Training carried out as on 7th. 28 ORs joined Battn from 53rd DRDB |
| 9-1-18 | Battalion less C Coy in Battn Areas. C Coy in Range Upon Lecture for all Officers W O's & N E O's in cohort. |
| 10-1-18 | Battn less D Coy in Battn Areas. D Coy in Range. 2-3pm. Officers under the C.O. in Tactical exercises. Subject - Attack & defence of a house or section of Village in which Battn is belleted. 5 pm Lecture by B.G.C in cohort |

2

|  |  |
|---|---|
| 11-1-18 | Rotation for D Coy as for 11th. D Coy on Range & O.R. from Bath. Band instructed in respirator drill. |
| 12-1-18 | Inter coy wiring Competition 1 NCO & 9 men from each Coy. Remainder engaged in "cleaning up". |
| 13-1-18 | R.C. Service held at 11-30. C.E. 11-30. A.M. T.R. C.O. inspected Coys as follows:- A & B 2-30 pm C & D 3-30 pm. Dress fighting order. |
| 14-1-18 | Coy Driving Teams reported to R.E. Instructor at Bolton Park (Capitaine Rousseau) |
| 15-1-18 | "C" Coy on Conversion Range. Demonstration Platoon under 2/Lt Russell carried out an attack on a strong point. |
| 16-1-18 | Programme of day cancelled owing to weather. Coys carrying out |
| 17-1-18 | do do do lectures & bathing parades. |
| 18-1-18 | Battalion Route march less 1 Platoon (see Coy 4) who paraded 10 A.M. for aeroplane defence as laid down for 17-1-18. Brigade Driving Competition. |
| 19-1-18 | R.E. Service 11 A.M C.E. 11-40 A.M |
| 20-1-18 | "B" Coy on Conversion Range. A = B = D. Coys carried out Coy work |
| 21-1-18 | Coys training as per programme |
| 22-1-18 | do do |
| 23-1-18 | Inter Athletes/Knockout 16th Brigade. |
| 24-1-18 | Training in P.T B.F.y Bar drill by Companies. All N.C.O's under the R.S.M. 1 hour. Foot drill carried out by O/C |

ARMY FORM C.2118

| | |
|---|---|
| 25-1-18 | 1 Platoon fired Coy on Canadian 3 Range M.A.R.A. Competition. Remainder of Battalion in following subjects:- B.F. Close order drill, Handling arms, Gas drill. Battalion feats A+D during hours curtailed and manoeuvres by night. |
| 26-1-18 | Interior Economy. |
| 27-1-18 | Church Parades arranged. |
| 28-1-18 | 1 Platoon per Coy on Canadian Range. Remainder of Battalion in following subjects:- Firing, close order drill, Rifle, Musketry Exercises, etc. |
| 29-1-18 | Training and Brigade Commander addressed the Battalion prior to engaging 146 Brigade Commander in wiring, and attacking a strong point in the presence of the Corps Commander. 3 Officers and 40 ORs crossed ground at 2/4 L.N.L.R. |
| 30-1-18 | No parades. 14 Officers and 241 ORs crossed. Bated to 14 L.N.L.R. |
| 31-1-18 | Annual Wiring Competition. 14 OFFICERS & 201 ORs, to ERQUINGHEM by lorries. Baggage & Transport Regiment comprising 520 OR remaining at ERNY-ST-JULIEN attached to 146 Brigade. |

27/1/18

J Walkrish
Capt.
for Lt Col Lemmy 1/5 L.N.L.R

www.ingramcontent.com/pod-product-compliance
Lightning Source LLC
Chambersburg PA
CBHW081424160426

43193CB00013B/2190